Best Sights to See at
White Sands National Park

By Rob Bignell

Atiswinic Press · Ojai, Calif.

BEST SIGHTS TO SEE AT WHITE SANDS NATIONAL PARK

A GUIDEBOOK IN THE BEST SIGHTS TO SEE SERIES

Atiswinic Press
Ojai, Calif. 93023
https://dayhikingtrails.wordpress.com

ISBN 978-1-948872-11-9

Cover design by Rob Bignell
Cover photo of gypsum dune at White Sands National Park
Back cover photo by Ann Vogl

Manufactured in the United States of America
First printing September 2020

For Kieran
"In your heart and your spirit let the breezes surround you/Lift up
your voice then and sing with the wind"
-John Denver, "Windsong"

Contents

Introduction

I magine a place where dunes of white sand rise taller than a house and seemingly forever into the horizon, where a trail's route shifts every day as wind remolds the terrain, where more than 800 animal species call an inhospitable desert home, where you can walk the shores of an ancient lake that mammoths and saber-toothed cats used to lap from. The place is real: It's called White Sands National Park.

But with the park's incredible size of nearly 228 square miles, how can you ensure that you see its main sights when vacationing or driving through? That's what "Best Sights to See at White Sands National Park" answers. In this volume, we've listed the park's top 7 most popular sights and experiences while detailing the top day hiking trails to best enjoy them.

Geology

The world's largest gypsum dunefield sits in southcentral New Mexico. At 275 square miles, about 4.5 billion short tons of white gypsum crystal make up the entire dunefield. White Sands National Park protects the southern half of the field. The dunes rise an average of 30 feet above the surface at White Sands, with the tallest dune about six-and-a-half stories high.

The sand dunes owe their creation to events from 251 million to 299 million years ago during the Permian. At the time, shallows seas covered this part of the world. When they receded, a seabed rich in gypsum was left behind. As the San Andres and Sacramento mountains rose, the gypsum was lifted to higher elevations. Rain dissolved the water-soluble gypsum, with rivers carrying the mineral down the mountains and depositing it in the basin below.

Fast-forward to the end of the last ice age, about 10,000 BC. Large lakes, streams and grasslands filled the Tularosa Basin between two mountain ranges. As the ice sheets retreated, weather patterns shifted, causing the basin to warm and dry out. One waterbody, Lake Otero, evaporated and became the alkali flat while the grassland turned to desert.

Exposed selenite crystals on the flat eroded into gypsum grains between 8000 and 5000 BC. Prevailing winds then blew the grains eastward, forming dunes, which stabilized about 2000 BC.

Geography

White Sands National Park sits at 4000 feet elevation in the Tularosa Basin. The 148,588-acre park protects 115 square miles of the gypsum dunefield with the rest of it in the White Sands Missile Range.

The dunefield is roughly crescent shape. Parabolic dunes make up the dune front, which forms the southern and eastern edge visible from U.S. Hwy. 70 and when first entering the park. Such dunes are U-shaped mounds trailed by elongated ridges and a shallow depression on the windward side. They form because strong winds there primarily are unidirectional.

Transverse-Barchan dunes sit behind them on the field's western and and northern sides. These arc-shaped dunes have gentle sloping sides on the windward side leading to high ridges with a steep dropoff on their front.

Dome dunes also can be found at the field's western edges, usually next to the park's Lake Lucero and the alkali flat. These dunes are large, rounded piles of sand.

A vast 1,600-square-mile alkali flat stretches between the dunefield's northwest side to the San Andres Mountains, which forms the basin's western wall. The flat is the remnant of the evaporated Lake Otero, which was larger than modern Rhode Island. Two connected pools that make up Lake Lucero are south of the alkali flat and west of the dunes. The lake often is dry, but after rain, snowmelt from the neighboring mountains, and upwelling from deep groundwater, it will fill, only for the water to quickly evaporate.

History

Humans have been in the area now compromising White Sands National Park for at least 12,000 years.

Based on fossilized footprints, Paleo-Indians inhabited the area around Lake Lucero about 10,000 BC. They lived among Columbian mammoths, ground sloths, ancient camels, bison, dire wolves, American lions, and saber-toothed cats. One track of fossil footprints suggests Paleo-Indians hunted a ground sloth there about 9700 BC.

After the region dried out and the dune field stabilized, a more advanced group known as "archaic people" settled in the region. They brought agriculture to the area about 2000 BC. Rather than spears, they used the atlatl. Their settlements included permanent villages.

The Jornada Mogollon people lived in the area between 200–1350 AD. These farmers used pottery and built adobe homes. They then migrated out of the basin. Exactly why they left is uncertain, but some archeologists believe it may be due to poor crop yields or lack of rain.

The Mescalero Apaches replaced them during the 1300s. Nomadic hunters and gatherers, the Apache bands followed bison herds from the Great Plains to the basin where White Sands sits.

During the 1500s, Spanish colonists settled near Sante Fe and generally avoided the Tularosa Basin because there were no reliable water supplies. In 1647, they established trails that touched a salt pan north of White Sands' alkali flats.

Two centuries later, Texan-American settlers entered the area and made private claims to land while the U.S. Army sent an expedition to establish a military wagon route. Hispanics formed farming communities elsewhere in the basin.

Apaches, led by Victorio and Geronimo, fought the colonists. In 1880, the Battle of Hembrillo Basin pitted Victorio's warriors against the U.S. Army's Buffalo Soldiers on what is now the White Sands Missile Range. Eventually the army forced the Apaches onto the Mescalero Apache Indian Reservation.

Ranching dominated the region from then on. Just east of White Sands, Holloman Air Force Base was established in 1942 and north of the area, the first atomic bomb was tested and exploded in 1945. Following the war, captured German scientists were sent to White Sands Missile Range to develop military rockets.

Calls to make White Sands a national park date to 1912. During the next decade, three such bills failed in Congress, though. Alamogordo businessman Tom Charles advocated for a national park during the 1920s and was successful in getting a state highway – which since has become U.S. Hwy. 70 – built through the area and passing the dunefield's southern edge. In 1933, White Sands was designated a national monument.

Since then, White Sands has been a popular place to film movies, especially westerns. Among the many well-known movies filmed here are *Four Faces West* (1948), *Hang 'Em High* (1968), *The Man Who Fell to Earth* (1976), and *Transformers* (2007).

During the 1970s, the New Mexico Department of Game and Fish introduced oryx to the basin for hunting. Having no natural predator, thousands of oryx came to reside on the missile range and soon entered White Sands, where they threatened native species by overgrazing. In 1996, the National Park Service erected a 67-mile fence to keep the oryx out of the park.

White Sands became a national park on Dec. 20, 2019, making it America's 62nd and newest national park. The redesignation added 2,029 acres to the park.

Park Layout

Trail access to the vast dune field is limited.

The northern half of the dune field sits in White Sands Missile Range with the western half of the park – which includes the alkali flat's southern portion, Lake Lucero and the dunefield's southwestern section – are shared by the missile range and national park.

The park itself marks the area accessible to the public. It consists of the dunefield's southcentral portion and some adjoining desert with a little bit of the alkali flat.

A single road – Dunes Drive – runs about 8 miles into the park, and all of the park's trails can be accessed from it. About nine miles of trails head into the dunes.

How to Get There

White Sands National Park is easy to reach from a variety of locations. The goal of any drive will be to reach U.S. Hwy. 70 either in Las Cruces or Alamogordo.

From Albuquerque and Denver, take Interstate 25 south to Las Cruces. From there, go east on Hwy. 70 over the San Andres Mountains to the Tularosa Basin.

From Tucson and Phoenix, drive Interstate 10 east to Las

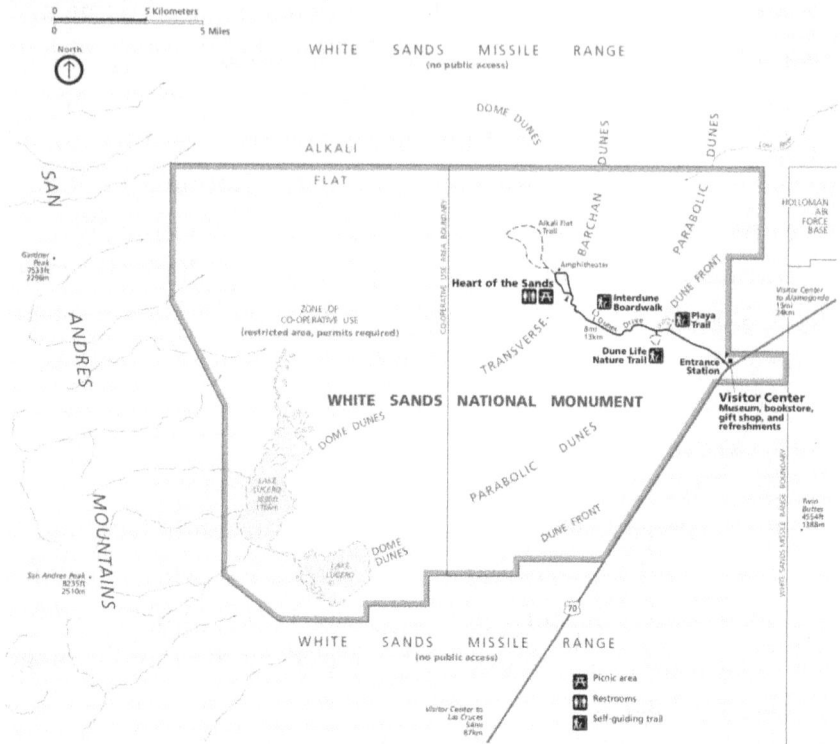

White Sands National Park (formerly White Sands National Monu-ment) sits in the Tularosa Basin between Alamogordo and Las Cru-ces. Illustration courtesy of White Sands NPS.

Cruces. Take Hwy. 70 east through Las Cruces into the basin.

From El Paso and San Antonio, follow Interstate 10 west to Las Cruces. Exit onto I-25 north and then Hwy. 70 east.

From Amarillo and Oklahoma City, go west on Interstate 40 to Santa Rosa, New Mexico. Exit south on U.S. Hwy. 54 and in Alamogordo head west on Hwy. 70.

Be forewarned that sometimes Hwy. 70 and even the park itself are closed because of tests conducted at White Sands Missile Range. Park and highway closures for tests are listed on the national park's website (*www.nps.gov/whsa/planyourvisit/*

park-closures.htm).

When to Visit

February through mid-May and mid-September through Thanksgiving mark the best times to visit White Sands National Park, as temperatures are fairly pleasant. Mid-May through mid-September can be unbearably hot with highs during June through early September hitting at least the high 90s. December and January can be cold with highs hitting only the 50s.

Kids Activities

A trip to White Sands National Park can be an educational experience for kids – though they may be having too much fun to even notice that they're learning!

The park delivers a variety of great activities that children can participate in all year long. Among the many offerings:

• **Adventure Packs** – Kids (via their parents) can check out backpacks at the visitor center for exploring the dunes. Each pack contains binoculars, compass, animal tracks fold-out guide, and several kid-friendly identification guides.

• **Junior Ranger Kids** – Kids can become a Junior Ranger. Parents first need to purchase a Junior Ranger booklet (available online and at the park visitor center), then children can complete its activities, and then they can receive a Junior Ranger patch or badge. One booklet is offered for preschoolers and another is for ages 6 and up.

• **Ranger-led events** – Programs at several locations throughout the park focus on a range of interests, from wildlife and plants found in the dunes and surrounding desert to preserving local natural and cultural treasures. Among the most popular programs are the Sunset Stroll, Full Moon Hike, and MothaPalooza.

Maps

To properly prepare for any hike, you should examine maps before hitting the trail and bring them with you (See the Bonus Section for more.). No guidebook can reproduce a map as well as the satellite pictures or topographical maps that you can find online for free. To that end, a companion website (*dayhik ingtrails.wordpress.com/trail-maps/*) to this book offers a variety of printable maps for each listed trail.

Best Sights

White Sands National Park is so large that unless you spend years there, you won't see all it offers. So when you've only a few days at best to visit the park, what are the absolute must-see sights? Following are the park's seven best spots and the day hiking trails for getting to them.

The Alkakli Flat Trail heads to a dry lakebed where wind gathers and blows gypsum to form White Sands' sparkling dunes.

Gypsum Dunes
Alkali Flat Trail

Day hikers can walk across the world's largest gypsum dunefield at White Sands National Park.

The 4.9-mile Alkali Flat Trail loops over the western portion of the New Mexico dunefield. It's one of the few trails in the world that requires a different route every time you hike it – the route changes daily as blowing winds remold the dunes.

To reach the trailhead, from U.S. Hwy. 70, take Dunes Drive into the park. As Dunes Drive circles back on itself, look for the parking lot on the road's west side. Do the trail counterclockwise.

The trail starts in a flat basin between dunes. After that, it's up and down the Transverse-Barhan Dunes.

Red fiberglass stakes with black arrows mark the way. The stakes are a must, as blowing sand would quickly obscure any path. They are about 300 feet apart, with signs every half-mile noting distances traveled, so the hike's route largely is a matter of playing dot-to-dot with the stakes.

Part of the trail's beauty is you get to decide how to best reach the next marker. A straight line usually isn't the smartest. Instead, follow the dune crests. Your feet will not sink into the sand as much on the dune's top as they would if going into a trough then back up the steep dune to the next crest. This turns the hike into a series of curves between markers.

Entering the dunes is a surreal experience, as pure white gypsum dunes and nothing else seemingly stretch forever before you. The only sight on the horizon are the hazy San Andres Mountains. You're actually crossing the narrowest portion of the dune field.

The white sand dunes cover 275 square miles of desert in the Tularosa Basin. Winds blowing off the San Andres sweep particles of gypsum off the Alkali Flats ahead and Lake Lucero to the southwest, forming the dunes.

Virtually no vegetation can grow in the gypsum dunes. On occasion, you will spot sumac bush, soaptree yucca, or clumps of grass, sitting on plant pedestals of hard, compacted sand that rises out the dune.

The dunefield's starkness is disorienting. Nothing but whiteness spreads around you, like you are lost in a snowstorm.

Still, as your eyes and mind get used to the dunes, you'll be able to notice some features.

Look out for footprints of fox and kangaroo rats. Soon you'll notice a lone beetle or lizard scampering about or a hawk soaring overhead.

Spotting the ground animals can be difficult. Mice, insects and lizards living on the gypsum dunes all use white coloration as camouflage. A product of evolution, the white versions of these creatures only appear in White Sands.

Stone ridges are another common feature. Thin, raised lines in the interdune flats, the gypsum here has solidified, marking the last spot the wind blew it. Gypsum is an ingredient in cement mix and used to make plaster and dry wall, so that it hardened in the natural world is not surprising. The stone ridges formed when heat removed water from the particles; when rain fell, the gypsum rehydrated and solidified.

A few gypsum pinnacles also can be found. The pinnacles formed in the same way as the ridges, but erosion has shaped them into fantastical shapes.

About a mile from the trailhead, the edge of the dunefield comes into sight. Beyond it is the trail's namesake, a 20-mile wide alkali flat. To the northwest, you'll also spot a few buildings and the water tower at the White Sands Missile Base's National Radar Cross Section Test Facility. On clear days, you also can see the hangars and buildings of White Sands Space Harbor, an alternate landing site for the defunct space shuttle.

In 2 miles, the trail reaches the last dune. Just 0.2 miles beyond it, the trail enters the dry lake bed, a remnant of ancient Lake Otero. A sign at the trail's western tip warns against going further because of unexploded ordnance. Part of the park is shared with the White Sands Missile Base, and sometimes the park and Hwy. 70 are closed for missile tests.

By this time, you've probably got a good amount of gypsum in your shoes and shoes. You may want to quick take them off and shake it all out.

Don't think of going barefoot on the way back, though. Gypsum is dry and abrasive, so walking barefoot across it for any length of time will leave your feet parched and cracked. On the plus side, unlike beach sand, gypsum isn't hot to touch and doesn't stick to you, so in those respects it's quite pleasant compared.

The trail soon circles back into the dunes. You're roughly a half-mile south of the route you walked in on.

The distant Sacramento Range looms ahead. These are much taller mountains than the San Andres, and snow can be on some of their caps even during summer.

If wind-blown sand proves too much for you, watch for "bowls" between the dunes. Here the dunes have left ground uncovered, and some desert scrub grows in them. The dune walls also provide some relief from the sand.

Sunscreen and sunglasses are a must on this trail, as the sand reflects the light in every direction. Sunglasses provide additional protection against blowing sand. Bring a lot of water, as well, at least 1.25 quarts per person. If you can't see the next red marker, turn back; getting lost on the dunes is easy.

Avoid the trail during the summer day, hiking it only very early in the morning or before dusk. Winter days are best for hiking this trail as highs reach the sixties. Spring usually means heavy winds as heat rises off the desert floor and cold descends from the San Andres. Regardless of the season, temps will drop in the evening by up to 30 degrees, which is a quite noticeable change in a dry climate.

Desert Wildlife

Dune Life Nature Trail

The vast, inhospitable gypsum dunes of White Sands National Park look lifeless to most visitors. Truth be known, more than 800 animal species call White Sands home.

A good way to learn about some of that wildlife is hiking the Dune Life Nature Trail. The 1-mile lollipop trail sits at the edge of the gypsum dunefield where it meets the surrounding desert scrubland.

Fourteen trailside signs tell about wildlife of both the desert and dunes. Even better, each placard has two parts – one for adults and one for kids – making this a great family trail.

To reach the trailhead, from U.S. Hwy. 70, enter the park on Dunes Drive. A turnoff on the left leads to a parking area for the trail, which leaves from the lot.

The trail's first 300 yards is the stem crossing the desert scrubland as approaching the dunefield. Then the route climbs steeply up a slope onto the white gypsum dunes and onto the loop.

From there, you'll have to walk through the soft sand. There is no marked trail on the ever-shifting dunes; instead, aim for the next marker.

As a transition zone between the dunefield and surrounding desert, there are more plants growing among the gypsum than you'll find deeper in the field. Yucca and grass clumps can be found here.

Along with the desert scrubland, all of this makes a nice home for a variety of wildlife.

You'll probably spot tracks for the kit fox, the largest animal that lives on the dunes. The size of a chihuahua, the kit fox weighs in at a mere five-pounds. Fur growing between its toes helps it maintain traction on the sand. It preys on kangaroo rats, Apache pocket mice, insects, lizards, and snakes.

Marriam's kangaroo rat isn't a marsupial but sort of looks like its Aussie namesake. Long, powerful hind legs allow it to jump 10 feet high. More than half of its 13-inch body consists of its tail, which it uses like a rudder to quickly change directions when chased.

Another animal that's adapted to living on the dunefield is the bleached earless lizard. Their coloration is white to match the gypsum, and they have no external ear openings for sand to blow into. They typically bury themselves under the dunefield's surface and feed on insects and spiders.

Most White Sands visitors are amazed to find that a couple of animals that are more associated with the northern forestlands also reside in the park.

The American badger lives on the dunefield's outer edges. Their long, powerful claws dig up burrows so they can capture reptiles, rodents and insects.

Porcupines are another surprise, though their numbers have diminished during the past few decades. They live in the scrublands on a diet of bark, buds and roots.

Thanks to the popular cartoon, most people associate coyotes and roadrunners with the desert, and White Sands has both.

Highly adaptable, coyotes prefer the desert scrublands but will go onto the dunefield if an opportunity for a meal presents itself. They'll eat just about anything, including road kill on the nearby highway.

The greater roadrunner – New Mexico's state bird – often can be seen darting about the park. This small creature can run up to 15 mph as it hunts lizards, rodents and snakes. It also can fly and uses elevated perches to search for prey.

Animals living at White Sands, like this bleached earless lizard, have evolved to belnd in with the gypsum dunes.

Birds make up more than a quarter of all animal species found at White Sands. In addition to owls and a variety of songbirds, the red-tailed hawk is quite common. With a wingspan of more than four-and-a-half feet and red-colored tail feathers, they usually can be spotted flying overhead searching for small mammals and reptiles to eat.

One good area on the dunes to spot wildlife is the hike's halfway point, where there's an interdune area of desert scrubland. Water flows into and collects in these bowls, allowing for plants – and hence animals – to thrive there.

Most animals are out at dawn or dusk, so those mark your best times to see any. Don't worry if you miss them, though, as there is a great view of the San Andres Mountains to the northwest to make up for it.

A couple of animals – or at least their tracks – to look for at the interdune area is the pocket gopher and the bobcat.

Pocket gophers primarily live in burrows but will come out to find a mate or dinner. If you see mounds or four wing saltbush and Indian rice grass, you can bet there's a maze of pocket gopher tunnels beneath your feet.

Badgers and coyotes usually dine on pocket gophers, but bobcats will too. The solitary, nocturnal cat ranges over several miles. The mostly stick to the dunefield's outskirts, but sometimes the flight of nesting birds will draw them to the interdune area.

From the interdune area, the trail ascends the second incline of the hike. The ascent is marked by a lone Rio Grande Cottonwood growing in the gypsum.

As the loop ends, it descends the dune and rejoins the stem crossing the desert scrubland.

Two kinds of rabbits make their home in the scrubland. The black-tailed jackrabbit can hit speeds of up to 40 mph, necessary if they are to escape their enemy the coyote. They don't burrow, however, so sometimes the coyote outlasts and catches them.

The desert cottontail, in contrast, likes to stay in burrows, though during cooler weather will come out during the day. They rarely stray far from their homes, as they are only half as fast as their black-tailed jackrabbit relative.

One other scrubland animal you might spot is the desert box turtle. A subspecies of the box turtle, it is adapted to living in the arid desert. It munches on small insects and plants.

Upon reaching your vehicle, be sure to check out the park's visitor center, which has displays about the dunefield's fauna.

There's no shade anywhere on this trail, so be sure to don sunscreen, sunglasses (the white gypsum dunes reflect sunlight far more than beach sand does), and sunhat. Bring plenty of water. If unable to see the next marker while on the dunes, turn back; you easily can get lost out there.

Playa
Playa Trail

Day hikers can explore a desert playa on a short trail. The 0.5-mile out and and back Playa Trail by far is the park's easiest hike. Utterly flat, it avoids the dune's deep sands that feet sink into. To reach the trailhead, from U.S. Hwy. 70 take Dunes Drive into the park. Leave your vehicle in the first pullout on the road's right side.

A playa is a low-lying area that fills with rainwater from storms. Most of the time, though, it is a dry lakebed.

The trail leaves from the pullout's center heading north into the Chihuahuan Desert scrubland at the edge of the vast gypsum dunes. In short order, it reaches the east side of a small playa and continues along its shore.

Playas are a common feature of deserts and there are several others at White Sands. Lake Lucero at 10 square miles is the park's largest playa and the current source of its gypsum sand. The playa on this trail, however, is the only one in the park that can be hiked, though sometimes ranger-led tours head out to Lake Lucero.

During summer, monsoon-like rains fill the playa with water. That instantly draws animals to it, and creates a lush new mini-ecosystem.

Even when the playa is dry, the area is not barren. A cryptobiotic crust grows around the playa atop the desert soil. The crust consists of lichens, algae and other microorganisms, and are the darker brown and black areas on the tawny sand.

Without this crust, the sandy soil never would have enough nutrients for other plants to grow. They also help stabilize the sand, and by doing so give plants a layer to take root in.

While the dry lake bed may be tempting to walk into, stay on

During the last ice age, the playa at the edge of today's gypsum dunes was a lush grasslands that many animals – including mammoths, saber-toothed cats, ground sloths, camels, and dire wolves – frequented.

the trail. Footsteps easily can damage the fragile cryptobiotic crust; in the harsh desert environment, it sometimes needs up to seven years to fully regenerate.

The Sacramento and Sierra Blanca mountains on the distant horizon emphasize how this is a land of extremes. Even in summer when temperatures on the desert floor top a 100 degrees, the highest point on the horizon, Sierra Blanca Peak, can be snow-capped. The peak is southern New Mexico's tallest mountain at nearly 12,000-feet elevation.

Five interpretive panels are located along the trail. At the end of the trail is one that imagines how this playa looked a mere 10,000 years ago at the end of the last ice age. The playa then was in a verdant grasslands, and giant creatures – Columbian mammoths, lions, ground sloths, dire wolves, camels and saber-toothed cats – all gathered at its shores. After taking in the sign, retrace your steps back to the pullout.

The trail is entirely exposed to the sun, so be sure to don sunscreen, sunglasses and sunhat. Though the route is short, always bring water.

Desert Flora

Interdune Boardwalk

Day hikers can amble down a boardwalk above the world's largest gypsum dunefield.

The 0.4 mile round-trip Interdune Boardwalk's flat aluminum "bridge" heads through a fragile interdune area. While plant life is sparse on the dunes, it flourishes in the lower spots between them.

To reach the trailhead, from U.S. Hwy 70 west go north onto Dunes Drive into the park. After 3.6 miles, turn right/north into a parking lot. The trail leaves from the lot's northwest side.

Ten signs along the boardwalk tell about the interdunal ecosystem. You'll probably spot animal tracks in the sands just off the boardwalk and certainly see plenty of flora.

Among the many plants visible from the boardwalk are soaptree yucca, little bluestem, Mormon tea, rubber rabbitbrush, little sand verbena, Gypsum centaury, and blazing star.

A long stalk rising high from a leafy shrub, soaptree yucca is the easiest to spot. If visiting in spring, watch for its large, cream-colored flowers. Native Americans dined on the yucca flower pods, used the leaves to construct rope and sandals, and boiled the roots to make soap and rugs.

Grasses thrive in the interdunal area. The prairie grass little bluestem is one such species. Because the water table is only a couple of feet below the surface at White Sands, the interdunal soils are moist, allowing the grasses to thrive. Alkali sacaton and Indian rice grass are two other grasses found at the park.

The short Mormon tea plant is spiny and stick-like, as if bamboo. Its leaves act as tiny scales. Each spring, pale yellow flowers bloom. It garnered its name from early pioneers who brewed a weak tea from its stems.

Plants often flourish in the low-lying spaces between the gypsum dunes.

During late summer, hundreds of golden flowers bloom and produce downy white seeds on the tall rubber rabbitbrush. Migrating butterflies flock to the gray-green shrub for food. Native Americans used the plant to make arrows shafts, baskets, and as a yellow dye.

The Gyp Nama, which grows only a couple of inches high, needs the sulfur in gypsum to grow, so the interdunal flats are a perfect habitat for it. They grow in tangled coils of thin green leaves with white edging, so look like a succulent plant; it's actually part of the waterleaf family.

Wildflowers also thrive in the flats. Gypsum centaury blossoms from April to October; the flower consists of five bright pink petals around a white center. Purple petals grow in tiny clusters on the little sand verbena while the blazing star looks like a yellow fireworks shooting out of a foot-high stalk.

The boardwalk ends with a viewpoint showing the dunefield and the mountain range beyond the valley floor. Sierra Blanca Peak stands out on the range's left side. Southern New Mexico's highest point, the usually snow-capped peak sits more than

7000 feet above the desert floor.

Note that the boardwalk's surface can be slick because of blowing sand. Also, avoid using the handrails unless you enjoy getting a shock due to static electricity buildup.

The trail is entirely exposed to the sun, so be sure to don sunscreen, sunglasses and sunhat. A structure offering shade is about midway along the boardwalk.

Wheelchairs and strollers will have no trouble using the boardwalk. Dogs are allowed on the trail but must be on a leash no longer than 6 feet.

White Sands boasts among the least light pollution of America's national parks, allowing visitors to see more 2000 stars in the night sky.

Stargazing
Backcountry Camping Trail

In most urban areas, artificial lighting and smog wash out the stars. Many people grow up only seeing a few of the brightest points in the night sky and never realizing the grandeur of the Milky Way that humankind has enjoyed for tens of thousands of years. But there still are places where one can see the night sky.

Among the darkest skies in America's national parks are at White Sands. For many who've never seen the night sky before, the sight is absolutely startling and awe-inspiring.

The park's 2.2-mile Backcountry Camping Trail is mainly for backpackers, but day hikers can take it as well while still light out. If backpack camping is your thing, though, this is an ideal trail for stargazing.

To reach the trailhead, from U.S. Hwy. 70 enter the park on Dunes Drive. Take the loop almost full circle. Just before coming back to Dunes Drive, enter the parking lot on the right/west. Leave your vehicle there.

There's no real trail – the ever-shifting sand prevents that. Instead, you'll follow orange-topped posts from point to point. The trail markers are set up with a 0.22-mile long stem and then a loop from it.

Trail heads up and down the dunes. Desert grasses, mesquite and yucca grow in the lower sections between the dune crests. Plenty of expansive, awe-inspiring views of the dune-field are to be had.

But if you really want to be awed, camp out in the dunefield and look at the starry sky. The least amount of light pollution in the park is in the middle of the dunefield, so on a moonless night, you'll be able to see more than 2000 stars.

The first delight is sunset. As the shadows deepen, the

dunes' brilliant white turns to tan then pink, purple, deep blue and finally gray as the sky becomes a black field of stars.

Stars by the season

What you'll see in the night sky changes with each season. Summer brings the spectacular band of the Milky Way, which is best seen on a moonless night. The Summer Triangle features the three bright blue stars, Vega, Altair and Deneb. Mid-August marks the Perseid Meteor Shower; park rangers usually hold a watch party for the meteor shower on another trail.

Autumn offers the Great Square of Pegasus, which rises in the northeastern sky at dusk. The Andromeda Galaxy is a fuzzy patch near the square. Autumn days are great for hiking the trail, but nights in the high desert can be cold.

Winter delivers the constellation Orion and the sky's brightest star, Sirius, which is only 8.6 light years from Earth. The red star Aldebaran is the winking eye in the constellation Taurus. While late winter can have pleasant days, nights will be very chilly.

In spring, two bright stars – orange Arcturus and blue Regulus – both are visible. The Big Dipper's handle points toward Arcturus, which appears near dusk in the eastern sky. To the south, Regulus is in the constellation Leo's front paw.

Stargazing pointers

Some quick tips for stargazing:

• **Go on moonless nights** – Reflecting sunlight to Earth, the moon can reduce the number of stars you'll see. Check the moon phases to find the perfect evening to stargaze.

• **Only use red lights** – The human eyes needs at least 20 minutes to adjust to low light. Bright non-red lights delay that process and can wash out the stars.

• **Layer your clothing** – The dry air at the higher elevations can make for nippy nights, even in summer. You'll probably need a sweatshirt and jacket on July evenings, though during the day you would roast alive wearing that.

• **Watch your step** – Animals come out at night, and you don't want to accidentally step on a snake or off a dune. All will end your stargazing adventure.

• **Bring a folding chair** – One that you can lean back in will reduce neck strain. Sitting in one spot, even if you adjust the chair slightly to see different parts of the sky, also will reduce the chances that you trample vegetation.

• **Carry water** – Many areas of the park have no running water. Even if not hiking, the dry air will cause you to feel parched.

Planning notes

A permit is required to backcountry camp at White Sands and can be purchased at the entry booths. They are given on a first come, first served basis. Only six people are allowed per backcountry campsite.

There is absolutely no shade, so be sure to don sunscreen, sunglasses and sunhat as well as bring plenty of water. If you can't see the next trail marker – which can occur thanks to blowing sand (especially in spring when visibility can be reduced to a few feet) or after heavy winds knock down a trail marker, return to the trailhead

Lastly, leashed dogs are allowed on the trail.

Visitors to White Sands can get an up close look at the park's wildflowers, like these Colorado four o'clock, on the Native Plant Garden Tour.

Wildflowers
Native Plant Garden Tour

Day hikers can enjoy desert flowers on the Native Plant Garden Tour at White Sands National Park.

The short trail – just 150-200 feet tops – is a self-guided walking tour in front of the visitor center. It's best seen mid-April through late November, as desert plants are dormant during winter.

To reach the trail, from U.S. Hwy. 70 enter the park via Dune Drives. Turn right/northeast on the very next road. Park in the lot and head northwest toward the visitor center entrance.

The visitor center was constructed during the mid-1930s in Spanish pueblo-adobe ("Pueblo-Revival") style using local materials. The center offers an excellent orientation film "A Land in Motion" about the national park. The 17-minute long film plays on the hour and half-hour.

At the visitor center information desk, you also can obtain a native plant garden guide for the walk.

White Sands sits at the northern end of the Chihuahuan desert. Plants growing there must be very durable because of the nutrient-poor soil and extreme temperature changes.

Start the walk by looking at the garden to right/east of visitor center door. Among the plants there are Apache plume, desert willow, Indian ricegrass, Colorado four o'clock, creosote bush, and to the right of White Sands sign, honey mesquite.

Of them, the Colorado four o' clock blooms from spring through summer. With showy purple to magenta blossoms, its five-lobed, funnel-shaped flower can grow up to two-and-a-half inches wide. It is found all across the American Southwest and northern Mexico.

The garden across from the Colorado four o'clocks contains three interesting desert plants – the three-leaf sumac, Torrey's jointfir, and soapatree yucca.

For visitors to New Mexico, the soaptree yucca will be the most noticeable because it's the absolutely alien looking. A long stem rises from a squat set of draping leaves. Large, cream-colored flowers bloom on the stem in late April through May.

Directly across the visitor center door is ocotillo and Torrey's Yucca.

Some desert plants bloom only after monsoon rains, and such is the case with ocotillo. Long, spiny cane-like stems rise from the shrub's short trunk. The stems can reach up to 20 feet high, as tall as a two-story building. When rain falls from March through June, dense clusters of red tubular flowers blossom from stems' ends.

The garden along the path behind this garden and next to the parking lot includes several desert plants. From northeast to southwest are New Mexico agave, lechuguilla, cane cholla, hoary rosemary mint, fourwing saltbush, purple prickly pear cactus, and desert spoon (also known as sotol).

Purple prickly pear cactus is a Southwestern icon. A shrub, it spreads by growing pad-like segments that turn shades of pinkish-purple. From April through May, its blooms open mid-morning, close at night, and never reopen. The flowers consist of yellow petals with its lower portions red, which form a brilliant red center.

The native garden lacks shade, so be sure to don sunscreen, sunglasses and sunhat. Sunburn can occur even after just a few minutes in the intense summer light.

Sledding
Heart of the Sands

Day hikers can sled during part of their walk at White Sands National Park.

Sledding on the snow-like dunes is a favorite activity of the park's visitors with most of them doing so in the Heart of the Sands area. There's not a trail exactly, but you'll do a lot of walking – all uphill – as you ascend the dunes and then slide down them.

Best of all, though, you can sled without stuffing yourself inside all of those bulky winter clothes.

To reach the sledding area, from U.S. Hwy. 70 enter the park on Dunes Drive. Once past the parking lot for the Interdune Boardwalk, vehicles are allowed to park off the side of the road.

While visitors often do this as soon as they see the first open dune to sled on, a much better choice is continuing to where the road loops, known as the Heart of the Sands area. This region will be less crowded, and there are actual parking lots. Any of the picnic areas are a good option. Being able to sled away from the main road also will be safer. The steepest dunes, however, are halfway along the loop as you begin heading toward the park entrance.

Unlike regular sand dunes, gypsum actually is great for tobogganing, as the firmer particles prevents the sled from sinking or piling up in front of you.

Unlike snow, which when compact turns to ice, the gypsum is not slippery. Because of this, sleds need to be waxed. Plastic saucers also tend to work best.

You can bring your own sled or purchase one at the gift shop back at the entrance. Wax for your sled also is available there in case you forgot it. If you slide down in the same spot several

Sledding on the gypsum dunes is a popular activity at White Sands.

times, that will create a smooth track, which reduces friction and so increases your speed.

The best kind of dune to slide is one with a gently sloping face and a level end. This allows you to come to a safe stop.

Take note of where the dune slope meets the desert floor. While the gypsum sand is soft, the base of the dune that is thin and touches the regular sand beneath can be extremely hard. Injuries have occurred.

Don't come to a stop in a roadway or a parking lot either. That will be just as hard as the desert floor with the added threat of moving vehicles.

Make sure there are no plants, sand clumps, or other obstructions in your sled's path. Besides destroying the fragile vegetation, you'll probably get scratched or cut up from sharp thorns, and those sand clumps can be like hitting concrete.

Sitting in the sled with your feet pointing downhill can make you more aerodynamic and increase your speed. Don't sled head first, though; while that still is fast, gypsum particles can more easily blow into your eyes, and should you crash, your noggin likely will take the brunt of the blow. Don't stand while sledding either, as you easily can lose your balance.

If little children are with you, they always should sled with an adult. Older children should be told about the various safety rules before allowed to hit the dunes.

Be sure to don sunscreen and sunglasses while sledding. The bright sun and reflection off the white sand will burn you quickly, and the all-white terrain will be blinding without eye protection.

Dripping Springs, in Oegan Mountains-Desert Peaks National Monument, is one of several great sights near White Sands National Park.

Nearby Sights

White Sands National Park sits amid a number of spectacular sights all boasting fantastic hiking trails. Most notable are the two mountain ranges surrounding the Tularosa Basin where White Sands is found. The Lincoln National Forest covers the range to the east of and largely overlooks Alamogordo. The Organ Mountains-Desert Peaks National Monument is to the west with part of it making for a stunning backdrop in Las Cruces. Many of those mountainous trails leave the desert for evergreen forests, and so deliver a quite different experience than at White Sands. There's also the Valley of Fires Recreation Area, a lava bed on the basin floor that is an impressive sight. If staying in either Las Cruces or Alamogordo, these nearby trails are easy day trips that are well worth the short drive.

The Malpais Nature Trail heads through a lava flow that covers 125 square miles in central New Mexico.

Valley of Fires Recreation Area

Malpais Nature Trail

Day hikers can explore a massive lava flow at Valley of Fires Recreation Area in eastern New Mexico.

The 0.9-mile Malpais Nature Trail loops through a small part of the 125-square-mile lava field. Sometimes the trail is referred to on maps and guides as the Valley of Fires Nature Trail.

To reach the trailhead, from Alamogordo take U.S. Hwys. 54/70 north. When the highways split, continue north on Hwy. 54. At Carrizozo, turn left/northwest onto U.S. Hwy. 380. Valley of Fires is on the left in about 4 miles.

The trail starts at the group shelter on the park road's northwest side. A paved trail, it features interpretive displays and has a handy guide brochure at the trailhead.

Before entering the lava field, the trail rises slightly to a sighting tube. Looking through it, you'll see Little Black Peak, the spot where the flow likely began some 5000 years ago.

Lava pumped out from that vent flowed some 44 miles across the Tularosa Basin. Ranging from 4 to 6 miles wide, the Carrizozo Malpais Lava Flow is as thick as 160 feet.

Continuing the trail toward the lava flow, in 0.13 miles, you'll reach the loop's start. Go straight/southwest to take the loop clockwise. In short order, you'll enter the lava field, a vast sprawl of black rock.

The lava flowed here in long, slow ropes called pahoehoe. Jagged blocks of lava, called a'a (pronounced ah-ah), also appear but are less common than pahoehoe.

Watch for large holes along the trail. When lava flowed here, these were the location of gas bubbles that collapsed as the surface cooled.

Plants and animals do thrive on the lava field. Bae grass, banana yucca, creosote, hedgehog cactus, mesquite, prickly pear cactus, sotol, walking stick cholla, and more – all common in the surrounding scrubland of the Chihuahuan Desert – have taken root in the flow's fissures and holes.

Living among these plants are desert cottontail rabbits, lizards, and various rodents, many of which have developed dark coloration as camouflage. A variety of birds – including golden eagles, great horned owls, harriers, ravens, red-tailed and Swainson's hawks, and turkey vultures – circle in the sky looking to make a meal of these creatures.

Other common birds in the lava flats are burrowing owls, cactus wrens, gnat catchers, quail, roadrunners, sparrows and towhees. Larger animals include barberry sheep and mule deer.

On the loop's northeast side is collapsed rock that probably was a lava tube at one time. These tubes formed when molten rock flowed beneath a surface of cool, hardened lava. Though not on the trail, there are eight intact lava tubes near Little Black Peak; four types of bats now roost in those "caves."

As the trail reaches the desert scrubland's edge, look for lava that curls back like a wave. Called kipuka, it formed when the lava flow hit a "shore" of higher ground, where the dirt and sandstone rock was cooler.

Once the loop reaches the stem trail, go left/northeast back to the group shelter.

Be sure to take it slowly so you don't trip on the trail. The lava is as sharp as broken glass and will cut you or your cloting. In addition, there's no shade at all on the trail, so be sure to don sunscreen, sunglasses and sunhat as well as bring plenty of water.

Lincoln National Forest
Cloud-Climbing Trestle Trail

Day hikers can explore two century-old trestle bridges on a short trail in New Mexico's Lincoln National Forest.

The 2-mile round trip Cloud-Climbing Trestle Trail is an old rail line converted to a hiking path. Brochures, maps and other guidebooks sometimes refer to it as the Mexican Canyon Trestle Trail.

To reach the trailhead, from U.S. Hwy 82 in Cloudcroft turn onto 24M to the Trestle Recreation Area. Leave your vehicle in the parking area.

Two trails lead from the loop's road into the rec area. The shorter of them and the preferred trailhead is on the loop's northwest side at the replica railway depot. The first half-mile is paved as winding through ponderosa pine and Douglas fir.

Decades ago, the trail marked the route of the former Alamogordo and Sacramento Mountain Railroad. The 32-mile route dropped nearly a mile in elevation to bring logged fir and spruce to sawmills in Alamogordo and mail and tourists both ways. It operated for almost a half-century from 1899 to 1947.

In about 0.1 miles, the trail junctions with the route that leads to the southwest corner of the rec area's driving loop. Continue right-straight/west.

First, though, pause at the Tularosa Basin Overlook. The vast desert valley covers 6500 square miles and is larger than Connecticut. White Sands National Park sits in the basin's southwestern section. Tobogan Canyon, which leads toward the basin, is to the overlook's south and west.

Another great vista awaits at 0.2 miles. The Devil's Elbow Overlook offers a fantastic view of the White Sands Missile Range on the desert floor below and the San Andres Mountains beyond. The overlook is near the large railroad cut known as

The ruins of an old trestle bridge for a rail line connecting the desert floor to the mountains awaits in Lincoln National Forest.

the Devil's Elbow, which was excavated in 1899 largely with hand labor and a little dynamite.

From the overlook, the trail turns sharply northeast. In a few yards, it joins the bicycle trail. Go right/northeast.

The trail next passes the remains of a 338-foot long, S-curved wooden railroad trestle. To support the heavy train, large timbers – some more than a foot square – had to be used. Originally this had another tier above the current highest one, and it once contained two 30 degree curves.

After the trail curls northwest, you'll come to one end of the S-Trestle. The trail turns to dirt in this area.

The forest here looks far different than it did when the railroad was constructed in the 1890s. A fire swept the area about a century ago, and aspen, a pioneer tree species, replaced the evergreens. White fir is now overtaking the aspen. Some of the white fir is immense, reaching up to 3 feet in diameter.

At roughly 0.6 miles, the trail splits upon coming to a bench. Continue right/northeast. Going left takes you to a trail shelter on the Old Cloudcroft Highway, which is used for ORVs.

Though the trail is popular, you stand a good chance of spotting deer and small forest critters. Elk and black bear sightings also are possible, but they usually stay farther away from town.

At 0.75 miles, another bench awaits as the trail zig-zags. In short order, the trail straightens and flattens.

The Mexican Canyon Trestle comes into sight at about a mile. The largest wooden trestle bridge at the time of construction, it measures 323-foot long and is the height of a six-story building. An overlook deck sits at one end of the trestle, and the area is a popular picnic site.

After taking in the trestle, retrace your steps back to the rec area parking lot.

Other Lincoln National Forest Trails

The Lincoln National Forest is divided into three distinct districts. The Sacramento Ranger District, located in the mountains above Alamogordo and surrounding Cloudcroft – is the closest to White Sands National Park and so receives the most attention here. The Smoky Bear Ranger District – located northeast of Alamogordo where Ruidoso is located – and the Guaudalupe Ranger District – southeast of Alamogordo on the New Mexico-Texas border – also contain some great trails, and a couple from each are listed.

Sacramento Ranger District

• **Alamo Canyon and Roundup Ground Trails** – A walk along a verdant canyon and around a prominent flat hilltop known as The Roundup Ground awaits hikers on this 6.6-mile lollipop trail. The route combines two trails, and hikers on it often report spotting desert wildlife. In Alamogordo, take White Sands Boulevard south and turn left/east onto Panorama Boulevard (which becomes Octotillo Drive) and then right/southeast onto Alamo Canyon Road. Park in the pulloff at the road's end.

• **Bridal Veil Falls & Grand View Trail** – Day hikers can head to a waterfall on this 7.3-mile lollipop trail, which climbs 793 feet in elevation. The trail starts in the desert, so it's best hiked September through May to avoid the heat. From Alamogordo, take U.S. Hwy. 89 east. Go left/north on Steep Hill Road then right/east on Fresnal Canyon Road. Park in the pullout at the trailhead, which is on the road's left/north side.

• **Dog Canyon Trail** – You can enjoy desert wildflowers and high rock walls as heading more than 1500 feet up the side of a canyon on this 10.2-mile round trip route. Walk it from September to May avoid the desert heat. For a less strenuous hike, go just 3.4 miles up the canyon for a 6.8-mile round trip that avoids the steep canyon wall. From Alamogordo, take U.S. Hwy. 54 south. Turn left/east onto Dog Canyon Road (aka Hwy. A16), and park where the road runs out at Oliver Lee Memorial State Park. The trail starts at the lot's northeast corner.

• **Lucas Canyon Trail** – A walk down a wildflower-filled canyon high in the Sacramento Mountains awaits on this 10-mile round trip trail with an elevation change of 1,610 feet. It's best done March to October to avoid snow. Horseback riding, mountain biking, motorcycle trail riding, and off highway vehicles also are allowed to use the trail. From Cloudcroft, take N.M. Hwy. 130 south/east. Turn left/southwest onto Russia Canyon Road. Park off the road at the trailhead.

• **Osha Trail** – A hike through a mountaintop forest awaits on this 2.5-mile lollilop trail just outside of Cloudcroft. It sports a 396 feet elevation gain at an already high altitude, but the fragrant scent of evergreens are payoff for all the effort. To avoid snow, hike it May to November. From downtown Cloudcroft, head west on U.S. Hwy. 82. Park in the lot at Muchachita Avenue intersection.

- **Switchback and Old Cloudcroft Highway Trail** – Hikers can walk on the remains of an old highway with 500 feet canyon walls above them. The 4.3-mile loop gains 515 feet in elevation. From Cloudcroft, take U.S. Hwy. 82 west. On the hairpin bend, turn right/north onto Bailey Canyon Road. Park on the side of the road after the Forest Road 206C intersection.
- **Willie White Trail** – Hikers can follow the route taken by old steam engines on this 5.2-mile trail that used to be a railroad grade. The trail runs between two points on County Road 17; you can extend the hike by adding the side Wills Canyon Trail. Horses and off-road vehicles also can use the trail. From Cloudcroft, take N.M. Hwy. 130 south/east. Turn right/southwest onto N.M. Hwy. 6563/Sunspot Highway. Go left/east onto Upper Rio Penasco Road. Park at the Bluff Springs campground.

Smoky Bear Ranger District

- **Cedar Creek Trail 120A** – Day hikers can enjoy a stroll through nature just outside the mountain resort town of Ruidoso on this 2.3-mile trail. Several stacked loops make up the Cedar Creek Trail system, but the one at the trailhead remains fairly flat with one brief climb up the canyon walls. From Ruidoso, take N.M. Hwy. 48 north. Turn left/northwest onto Cedar Creek Drive. A parking lot with the trailhead is the first right.
- **Grindstone Lake Loop** – Hikers can walk along three sides of a mountain lake on this 6.7-mile trail. Grindstone Lake sits at 6890 feet elevation, nestled at the bottom of a mesa. The trail also ascends the mesa side, offering some challenging

climbs and cool switchbacks. Much of this loop was built in 2013. From N.M. Hwy 48 in Ruidoso, take Fifth Street west. Turn right/south onto Resort Drive. The third left/west heads to a parking lot alongside the lake and the trailhead.

• **Park Ridge Trail** – Hikers can head up to a ridge overlooking Ruidoso on this 5-mile loop. It spots a 650-foot elevation gain, but the views and chance of seeing local wildlife makes the hike worth the effort. Horse riding and Leashed dogs are allowed on the trail. From Main Road in Ruidoso, turn north onto Ebart Drive then left/northwest onto Perk Canyon Drive, left/west on Echo Drive, left/south on West Rednord Drive, and right/northwest onto Perk Canyon Drive. The trailhead is near the curve where the street becomes Thunderbird Drive.

Guaudalupe Ranger District

• **Anderson Canyon Trail** – Hikers can walk through the Chihuahuan Desert on this easy to reach 1.3-mile out and back trail. The last portion of the trail runs alongside an intermittent stream. From Carlsbad, take U.S. Hwy. 285 north. Turn left/west onto N.M. Hwy. 137 then right/north on the road to the Guadalupe Administrative Site and park in the first pullout on the left. Follow the road north to the trail, which maps and brochures also refer to as T68E.

• **Sitting Bull Falls Trail** – A waterfall awaits at the end of this 3-mile trail, which leaves from the Sitting Bull Falls Recreation Area, a desert oasis. The falls drops 150 feet from what looks like a hanging garden. Restrooms and picnic tables are near the trailhead. From Carlsbad, take U.S. Hwy. 285 north. Turn left/west onto N.M. Hwy. 137 then right/southwest onto County Road 409. The road ends at a parking lot in the rec area.

Organ Mountains-Desert Peaks National Monument

Indian Hollow Trail

Day hikers can enjoy fantastic views of spires and the desert basin below on the Indian Hollow Trail at New Mexico's Organ Mountain-Desert Peaks National Monument.

The 5-mile out-and-back trail is not for the inexperienced hiker, as it gains 1893 feet elevation at a high altitude. Good hiking boots are required, as loose rocks abound on the trail.

To reach the trailhead, from U.S. Hwy. 70 between Las Cruces and Alamogordo, go south on Aguirre Springs Road. Drive 6.1 miles to a turnoff for the trailhead, which is northeast of the Aguirre Springs Group Area. Park at the road's end.

The trail begins at about 5450 feet above sea level with a gentle ascent. In short order, the trail crosses Sotol Creek then turns sharp east.

Because the trail climbs bare rock and goes up and down some drainages, some hikers have had difficulty staying on the trail. Watch for cairns to keep you on the route. More importantly, practice tried and true navigation techniques by frequently checking your map and compass, aiming for a point, and once there repeating that step.

About halfway through the hike, the trail crosses a stream (the third stream you'll head over) then parallels it and a tributary. Cottonwoods and pines line the creeks. This is a great area for birding.

From there, the trail begins a steep ascent up a dividing ridge. After crossing the tributary, the trail sits below the Organ Needle's soaring walls on the west and Sugarloaf Peak to the west.

About a fifth of a mile from the tributary, the trail peters out.

The Indian Hollow Trail travels high into the Organ Mountains overlooking White Sands.

You're at about 7340 feet elevation.

The reward for all the effort is the jaw-dropping views.

To the northeast is White Sands Missile Base and beyond that the sprawling dunes of White Sands National Park. The major needles of the Organ Mountains are to the east. The Needles is the northernmost of them at 8416 feet high while the Organ Needle is the southernmost at 8885 feet.

Sugarloaf Peak, shrouded in Douglas firs, Gambel's oaks, and pines, is to the southeast, topping out at 8015 feet. If you look close enough, you'll probably spot tiny figures hiking to its top.

On the walk back to the trailhead, Rabbit Ears peak sits to the northwest at 8006 feet. Baylor Peak is beyond it at 7668 feet.

During winter, snow often is on the trail, and by autumn, it can be overgrown in spots. It's best hiked during spring early in the morning to avoid the midday heat. As parts of the trail are not shaded, be sure to don sunscreen and sunglasses. Leashed dogs are allowed on trail.

Other Organ Mountains-Desert Peaks National Monument Trails

Organ Mountains-Desert Peaks National Monument is a great destination for hikers in the Las Cruces area. Located west of and partially visible from White Sands National Park, the 496,330-acre national monument offers a plethora of pre-historic, historic, geological and biological treasures to enjoy.

The national monument consists of four general areas: the Organ Mountains; Desert Peaks; the Doña Ana Mountains; and the Potrillo Mountains.

Organ Mountains

This steep mountain range rises off the desert floor to 9000 feet above sea level, delivering a number of pointed peaks, narrow canyons, and ponderosa pine woodlands to explore.

• **Achenbach Canyon Trail** – Great views of the Organ Mountains await on this 5.5-mile route southwest of Las Cruces. It sports an elevation gain of 1,272 feet to a walking trail known as Soledad Canyon Road. From Interstate 25 and University Avenue in Las Cruces, take the latter east. University becomes Dripping Springs Road. Turn right/south onto the street Soledad Canyon Road then right/south onto Ladera Canyon Road. The trailhead is on the left/east in about about 0.6 miles. Leashed dogs are allowed on the trail.

• **Bar Canyon Trail** – Hikers can explore the ruins of an 1800s ranch in the Organ Mountains' western foothills on this 1.3-mile trail. Located in the Soledad Canyon Day Use Area, mule deer usually can be spotted grazing in the canyon. From Interstate 25 and University Avenue in Las Cruces, take the latter east. University becomes Dripping Springs Road. At Soledad Canyon Road, go right/south. Parking and the trailhead are at the road's end.

• **Baylor Canyon Pass Trail** – Hikers can head from desert foothills to tree-covered terrain at a mountain pass on this 6.3-mile out and back trail. There is a 1548-foot elevation gain. From Interstate 25 and U.S. Hwy. 70 in Las Cruces, take the latter east toward Organ. Turn right/south onto Baylor Canyon Road. The parking lot and trailhead is on the left/east. A day use pass is required, and dogs are allowed.

• **Dripping Springs Trail** – Day hikers can see a rare waterfalls in the desert on this moderately challenging 2.7-mile trail. Because of the lush environs, this trail also is great for bird-watching. From Interstate 25 and University Avenue in Las Cruces, take the latter east. University becomes Dripping Springs Road. Park at the A.B. Cox Visitor Center; the trail heads southeast from it. A fee is charged for parking and no dogs are allowed.

• **Fillmore Canyon Trail** – A 40-foot waterfall awaits at the end of a canyon in this 2.1-mile out and back trail. Fillmore Falls is narrow but thanks to being spring-fed runs year-round. From Interstate 25 and University Avenue in Las Cruces, take the latter east. University becomes Dripping Springs Road. Park at the La Cueva Picnic area, from which the trail heads northeast.

• **La Cueva Trail** – A cave that has been inhabited for at least 5000 years sits at the end of this 1.1-mile out and back trail. The rock shelter also is known as the Hermit's Cave. From Interstate 25 and University Avenue in Las Cruces, take the latter east. University becomes Dripping Springs Road. Park at the A.B. Cox Visitor Center; the trail heads northwest from it across the former Hayner Resort Airstrip. A fee is charged for parking and dogs are not allowed.

• **Mine House Spring Trail** – Ruins of a former mountainside mine await hikers on this 3.6-mile out and back trail. At one time, the Hayner Ruby Mine drew fluorite from the rock beneath the Rabbit Ears. The trail boasts a 1,072-foot elevation gain, and dogs are allowed. From Interstate 25 and U.S. Hwy. 70 in Las Cruces, take the latter east toward Organ. Turn right/south onto Baylor Canyon Road. Shoulder parking and the trailhead is in about five miles. The trail often is shown as Topp Hut Road on maps.

• **Organ Needles Trail** – Hikers can head across the desert valley then up to Needles Peak on this 5.8-mile out and back trail. It is a very difficult hike meant only for experienced hikers who are in good shape, as the trail sports a 3,562-foot elevation gain. From Interstate 25 and University Avenue in Las Cruces, take the latter east. University becomes Dripping Springs Road. Park at the La Cueva Picnic area, from which the trail heads northeast. Dogs are not allowed, and hikers should carry additional water.

• **Pine Tree Trail** – Hikers can explore the base of the Needles foundation in the Aguirre Springs section of the Organ Mountains on this 4-mile lollipop trail. Be sure to bring water; there are no springs. From Las Cruces, take U.S. Hwy. 70 east to Organ. Turn right/southeast onto Aguirre Springs Road. When the road loops, the parking lot and trail is on the far side just past the Aguirre Springs Campground. A parking fee is required, and dogs are allowed on the trail.

• **Rabbit Ears Plateau Trail** – Hikers can clamber to one of the points on the Rabbit Ears formation via this 6.1-mile out and back trail. Because of the 2,893 feet elevation gain in a

desert environment, this trail is recommended only for experienced, fit hikers. From Interstate 25 and U.S. Hwy. 70 in Las
Cruces, take the latter east toward Organ. Turn right/south onto Baylor Canyon Road. Shoulder parking and the trailhead are
on the left/east in about 4 miles.

• **Sierra Vista Trail** – Hikers can walk along the base of the
Organ Mountains on this 29-mile one-way trail connecting Las
Cruces and El Paso. Creosote, ocotillo and cacti – a well as wildlife in the remote sections – abound along the trail. As the trail
is entirely on the floor of the Chihuahuan Desert, it is best
avoided during summer. From Interstate 25 and University
Avenue in Las Cruces, take the latter east. University becomes
Dripping Springs Road. Watch for the parking lot and trailhead
on the road's right/south.

• **Sugarloaf Peak Trail** – Unless a rock climber, hiking to
the top of the prominent Sugarloaf Peak granite dome isn't
pos-sible. Day hikers can get close, however, by walking 6
miles round trip to a large semicircular depression, known as
the "eye," on the mountain's side. The eye sits at 7500 feet elevation, about 515 feet below the monolith's summit. From U.S.
Hwy. 70 between Las Cruces and Alamogordo, go south on
Aguirre Springs Road. Drive 6.1 miles to a turnoff for the trailhead, which is northeast of the Aguirre Springs Group Area.
Park at the road's end and start on the Indian Hollow Trail then
take the spur to Sugarloaf Peak.

• **Tortugas Mountain Trail** – Hikers can take a loop on the
mountain sporting a large A in tribute to New Mexico State's
Aggies on this 3.9-mile route. Though rocky at times, the trail
offers great views of the Organ Mountains and the Mesilla Valley. From Interstate 25 and University Avenue in Las Cruces,
take the latter east. University becomes Dripping Springs Road.
At Sonoma Ranch Boulevard, go right/south. A parking lot and

trailhead are at the road's end.

Desert Peaks
   Several mountain peaks in this part of New Mexico rise directly off the desert plain. Among them are the Robledo Mountains and Sierra de las Uvas.
   • **Picacho Peak Trail** – A fantastic view of the Mesilla Valley and the Organ Mountains awaits on this 2.2-mile trail round trip trail that heads to the top of a 35-million-year-old volcanic mountain. The trail gains 764 feet on its way to the 4959-foot high peak. From the junction of Interstate 10 and West Picacho Avenue/U.S. Hwy. 70 (Exit 135), take the latter east. Turn north on Picacho Hills Drive and after a mile continue on Barcelona Ridge Road. Go north on Anthem Road then turn north onto the unpaved Loop Road. The trailhead parking lot is in 1.5 miles.
   • **Prehistoric Trackways Trail** – The world of 280 million years ago is preserved along this 7.8-mile trail, which features footprints of reptiles, amphibians and insects as well as fossils of plants and petrified wood. Though actually part of the Prehistoric Trackways National Monument, the 5280-acre site sits in the Robledo Mountains next to the Organ Mountains-Desert Peaks National Monument. The trail boasts 1,459 feet in elevation gain, and leashed dogs are allowed on it. From the junction of Picacho Avenue/U.S. Hwy. 70 and Shalem Colony Trail in Las Cruces, take the latter north. Turn west on Rocky Acres Trail to the trackways' dirt road entrance on the left/west. Only high-clearance, 4wd vehicles can traverse the road after a mile.

Doña Ana Mountains
   Though one of the desert peaks its own right, this area

usually is considered separate because of its distance from the other such summits. It also boasts extensive recreational facilities for hikers, mountain bike enthusiasts, rock climbers and equestrians.

• **Dona Ana Peak Trail** – Hikers can head up a canyon and scramble over rocks on a 1.7-mile round trip trail to a mountain peak at 5822 feet above sea level. The trail gains 977 feet in elevation as passing cacti and yucca while hawks and owls fly overhead. From the junction of U.S. Hwy. 70 and Sonoma Ranch Boulevard, take the latter north. Turn right/east onto Peachtree Hills Road then left/north onto DO64/Jornada Road. Go left/west onto DO63. In 1.7 miles, turn left/south onto an unpaved road. Turn right/west in 2.7 miles onto another unpaved road; the trail begins where the road ends.

Potrillo Mountains

Located southwest of Las Cruces, this remote section consists of cinder cones, lava flows, and volcanic craters.

• **Kilbourne Hole Volcanic Crater Trail** – You can hike the rim of a maar volcanic crater that is at least 24,000 years old on a 7.8-mile loop. The crater measures 1.7 miles long by a mile across and is hundreds of feet deep. It's located in the Kilbourne Hole Volcanic Crater National Natural Landmark, adjacent to the Organ Mountains-Desert Peaks National Monument. From the junction of Interstate 10 and New Mexico Hwy. 183/ Vinton Road, take the later west. Go right/south on New Mexico Hwy. 28/Lew Henson Highway then right/west onto New Mexico Hwy. 182. Next turn right/ north onto Alvarez Road and then left/northwest onto A020. Go left/southwest onto Aviation Road. Upon crossing the rail-road tracks, take A012 right/north then A011 left/west. At the junction of A013, pull off the road and follow the first path north to the crater rim.

Farther Afield

For travelers driving a distance to White Sands, there are plenty of great sights along the way that you ought to make a side trip to see. Among the two biggest are Saguaro National Park if coming coming west from Tucson and the adjacent Carlsbad and Guadalupe Mountains national parks if coming east from southern Texas. Another excellent hiking area between Tucson and White Sands is southeast Arizona's Chiricahua National Monument. All offer quite different experiences than White Sands, adding a variety of unique, fantastic hikes to your trip.

Carslbad Caverns sits 70 stories underground in an ancient coral reef.

Carlsbad Caverns National Park
Big Room Trail

A hike through a cave will delight any child – especially when it's one as spectacular as Carlsbad Caverns. Massive stalagmites and stalactites, a bottomless pit, a reflective pool hundreds of feet beneath the surface and more all await visitors.

Another bonus: Carlsbad Caverns can be enjoyed any time of the year – the cave's temperature varies little from its 56 F temperature, making it a nice respite from both the summer heat or a Northern winter cold. Regardless of the season, you'll need a light jacket or sweatshirt when underground. Comfortable shoes with good traction also are a must.

To reach Carlsbad Caverns, you'll have to cross what looks like a scene out of the Old West. Agave and paddle cactus line the desert highway of U.S. Hwy. 62/180 that links El Paso and Carlsbad, N.M. For miles, there's not much to see but beautiful open desert country, and then the cavern's visitor center with its expansive parking area suddenly rises out of the emptiness.

With younger children, you'll want to limit your hike to the Big Room tour. Elevators in the visitor center take you 754 feet underground, depositing you at a rest area and lunchroom. Look for the signs to a wide passage that leads you to the massive Big Room, which is 3,800 feet long and 600 feet wide. The relatively level and well lighted 1.25-mile self-guided trail heads counter-clockwise around the chamber.

Carlsbad Caverns are in the remnants of what once was a 400-mile long reef on an inland sea that covered North America about 250 million years ago. As the sea evaporated, salts and gypsum buried the reef. Uplift and erosion began exposing the buried rock a few million years ago. Slightly acidic groundwater and rain seeped through the rocks, carving out the fantastic caverns and its incredible formations.

Among the first of those features on the Big Room trail is the Hall of Giants. The limestone Giant Dome soars 62 feet high and at 16 feet in diameter is wider than most trees. Many visitors say it resembles a miniature Leaning Tower of Pisa. Next to Giant Dome sit a pair of limestone structures aptly named Twin Dome. White lighting allows you to see their natural colors.

Further up the trail is the Temple of the Sun, an elegant limestone formation that almost appears to be handcrafted, surrounded by stalactites above and stalagmites below. There's a bench nearby for taking a rest.

Next is Caveman Junction, featuring a rock formation that vaguely looks like a Neanderthal (though they never lived in North America). If young children with you are frightened of the cave or some other problem arises, turn left here for a shortcut to the other side of the looping trail.

If continuing on the trail, next is the Totem Pole, a long skinny rock formation that stretches far above your heads. Then comes a view of Lower Cave, which is lit with green lights. After that is the Top of the Cross, named because of its position given the room's shape.

Among the two most intriguing sights on the trail follow. Mirror Lake is an illuminated pool, and the Bottomless Pit stretches 370 feet deep. Warning: Along the main trail are many closed gates guarding small paths leading to unseen passages; children shouldn't wander off the trail into these gated areas.

Next is Crystal Spring Dome, a wet cone-shaped stalagmite that still is growing. Note the dark brown spot – it is caused by people touching it, even though they shouldn't as it damages the structure.

Near the trail's end is the Rock of Ages, an impressive formation that looks like the hand of God had placed it there. Then comes the Painted Grotto, an array of calcite speleotherms and soda straws with iron oxide staining.

Take the Jim White Tunnel (the parking lot is some 50 stories directly above you) back to the rest area.

Other Carlsbad Caverns National Park Trails

Among the best ways to see Carlsbad Caverns National Park's major sights is via a day hike. Though the park is vast, three short trails will allow you to enjoy the park's major highlights – the massive underground cave, a bat flight like no other, and rugged desert scenery.

Caverns

Rather than take an elevator to the cavern, hikers can use the natural entrance and walk 75 stories underground. It's a great adventure for those who want to see Carlsbad Caverns just as early explorers did. Sights along the way are include Devil's Spring, the Whale's Mouth, and Iceberg Rock. The **Natural Entrance Trail** runs 1.25 miles.

Bat flight

Every sunset from June through October, hundreds of thousands of bats fly out of Carlsbad Cavern's natural entrance in a tornadic-like spiral to feed for the evening then return at dawn. The **Chihuahuan Desert Nature Trail**, a half-mile loop, allows you to watch the bats disperse across the New Mexican desert.

Desert scenery

With intriguing rock formations, a lush dry run, and great vistas of the plains below, Yucca Canyon offers the most scenic aboveground trail in the park. The **Yucca Canyon Trail** runs seven miles out-and-back to the canyon's top, gaining 1500

Each evening at dusk, hundreds of thousands of bats fly out of Carlsbad Caverns through the natural entrance.

feet elevation gain. From U.S. Hwys. 61/180, go west on County Road 418; the trailhead is on the road's left side just after entering the park.

Guadalupe Mountains National Park
Guadalupe Peak Trail

Hikers can head to Texas's highest point at Guadalupe National Park.

The Guadalupe Peak Trail climbs 3,000 feet to the 8,749-foot summit in an 8.5-mile round trip. It's a strenuous hike across rocky ground, but the views of neighboring El Capitan and the Chihuahuan Desert below are worth the workout. Because of the high altitude, plan 6-8 hours for the hike.

To reach the trailhead, from the El Paso metro area, take U.S. Hwy. 180 east. Upon reaching the park, turn left/northwest onto Pine Canyon Road. Check in at the Pine Springs Visitor Center then follow Pine Canyon Road to its end, where there's a parking lot. The trail leaves from the lot's northwest corner.

At 0.7 miles, the trail junctions a horse path that also goes to the peak. You'll want to take the hiker trail. You can take the horse trail, of course – it's not as steep, but the tradeoff is it's a mile longer.

Switchbacks head up the hiker trail's first 1.5 miles as ascending a steep slope. Increasingly great views of the desert below appear the higher you go.

Guadalupe Peak and the rest of this mountain range began to form some 261 million to 299 million years ago. At that time, this part of the world was under a shallow sea. Conditions were right for coral reefs to grow in an arc some 600 miles long. Called the Capitan Reef, it is one of the world's best preserved ancient reefs.

Around 260 million years ago, the sea where the reefs grew began to evaporate. Minerals settled to the sea floor and mixed with new sediment flowing into the basin eventually covered the reefs. Over the eons, it hardened into rock.

After the switchbacks, the trail passes a cliff and reaches the

Topping out at 8749 feet, Guadalupe Peak is Texas's highest point.

mountains' north-facing slope. A small forest of pinion pine, southwestern pine, and Douglas fir thrives there due to less sunlight from the north and hence a cooler environment than on the mountain's other slopes.

The trail reaches a false summit about 3 miles in. A sparse ponderosa pine forest covers this flat spot. At 3.25 miles is a backcountry campsite.

Texas and New Mexico slowly began to rise in elevation about 80 million years ago. Faults formed along the range's western margin, causing the Capitan Reef to rise several thousand feet. During the past 20 million years, erosion from wind and rain has carved the Guadalupe Mountains into their current shape.

The trail next descends a bit and crosses a wooden bridge.

From there, the final ascent to the summit begins.

After going up a few switchbacks, the top of nearby El Capitan dominates the southern skyline. You're almost there once the trail passes the horse hitching posts.

The trail reaches the summit at 4.25 miles. A triangle monument, erected in 1958, commemorates overland stage and air travel and marks the summit. You can sign a register there to show you're part of the elite club that has reached the top of Texas.

From the summit, several peaks in the Guadalupe Mountains are visible. To the northwest, Bartlett Peak rises to 8498 feet while Bush Mountain soars behind it to 8616 feet. Hunter Peak is to the northeast at 8258 feet. El Capitan is directly south at 8065 feet.

Upon taking in the sights, retrace your steps back to the parking lot.

Much of the trail's base and certainly its peak are exposed to sun and wind, so be sure to don sunscreen, sunglasses and sunhat. A good pair of hiking boots and a trekking pole are highly recommended. Carry at least 3-5 liters of water per person. If noticing signs of altitude sickness, turn back; there really is less oxygen on the peak.

Other Guadalupe Mountains National Park Trails

Among the best ways to see Guadalupe Mountains National Park's top sights is via a day hike. Just four short trails will allow you to enjoy many of the park's highlights – an old stage coach station, a maple-filled canyon in the middle of the desert, gypsum sand dunes, and a fossilized coral reef.

Butterfield Stage station

Along the Texas-New Mexico border, families can step back

into the Old West and experience the remoteness of what once was a welcome sign to travelers: a Butterfield Stage station in the Guadalupe Mountains. The 0.75-mile round trip **Pinery Trail** marks a great day hike for families at Guadalupe National Park. The trail leads to the ruins of the Pinery Station, a once favored stop on the original 2,800-mile Butterfield Overland Mail Route.

Scenic McKittrick Canyon

Filled with bigtooth maple trees, the canyon and its intermittent stream are beautiful in fall when the leaves blaze orange to red. The **McKittrick Canyon Trail** runs 4.8 miles round-trip through the canyon to Pratt Lodge.

Gypsum sand dunes

On the west side of the national park near Dell City, bright-white gypsum sand dunes cover more than 2000 acres and rise up to 60 feet high. From the end of Williams Road, follow the **unnamed trail** in a 1.2-mile round trip walk across desert to the dunes.

Fossilized coral reef

Some 251 to 299 million years ago, this section of the world sat under a sea. As the plants and animals died, their remains formed an erosion-resistant limestone reef that now makes up the Guadalupe Mountains. The **Permian Reef Trail** rambles 8.4-miles round trip past many of the reef's geological wonders. The trail does gain 2,000 feet of elevation.

Gila Cliff Dwellings National Monument
Gila Cliff Dwellings Trail

Day hikers can explore an ancient cliff dwelling on a remote trail in southwestern New Mexico.

The 1.1-mile lollipop Gila Cliff Dwellings Trail sits in the Gila Cliff Dwellings National Monument near Pinos Altos. You'll gain 180 feet elevation as climbing from the river valley through Cliff Dweller Canyon.

The cliff dwellings are off the beaten path, as you'll drive a long, winding mountain road to get here. The scenery along the way and the trail at the national monument are worth it, though. To reach the trailhead, from Silver City simply take N.M. Hwy. 15 north. Plan for this drive to take a lot longer to than you'd expect, as it can't be done at 55 mph. The road literally ends at a parking lot with the trailhead on the southwest corner.

Though the trail is short, you'll cross four different ecological zones – riparian, canyon, desert and forest. The trail begins in the riparian river area with a bridge over the West Fork Gila River.

After crossing the river, the loop starts. Go left/south on it. The trail heads up a canyon that shade trees and a creek keep cooler than the surrounding, sun-exposed cliffs.

About a quarter-mile into the hike, you'll come to a viewpoint of the cliff dwelling. This is about the best spot to get a photo of the entire set of dwellings.

Continuing on the loop, the next 180 feet will be steep. After looping around to the trail's west side, the route is more manageable.

At last, the trail arrives at the cliff dwellings. Gila Cliff is one of the few parks that allows visitors to enter cliff dwellings, so take this opportunity.

Forty-two rooms that were occupied about 700 years ago make up the Gila Cliff Dwellings.

The dwellings are in fairly good condition given that they were constructed 700 years ago. Even the wood used in the original construction remains. Six alcoves in all make up the structure.

Entering the dwellings, you can go through several of the 42 rooms. They are mostly empty, and some can be accessed only by ladder, but it's fascinating, nonetheless.

The ancient Puebloan of the Mogollon area built the dwellings between 1260 and 1280 CE. In the river valley below their dwellings, they grew fields of beans, corn and squash and on the surrounding mesa hunted wild game while gathering wild edible plants. They also made beautiful, distinctive pottery.

Why they abandoned the area by around 1300 CE is unclear,

but archeologists suspect climate changes briefly dried out the area.

The trail next heads through the cliff's desert-like slopes back to the base of the canyon. Watch your step on the loose gravel and uneven stone steps.

Rising around the canyon is a pine and fir forest. The trail heads through some of this on the way back to the parking lot.

The park typically is open at 9 am to 5 pm, except on Christmas and New Years Day, and visitors are not admitted after 4 pm. No food or gum is allowed on the trail. An on-site kennel for pets is available. Cell phones do not work anywhere on or near the trail.

Other Gila Cliff Dwellings National Monument Trails

There's much more to see at the Gila Cliff Dwellings than the spectacular ancient ruins. Hot springs, river valley vistas, a pictograph panel, and riverside walks all await day hikers. Among the trails to see those sights are:

• **Middle Fork Trail** – Hikers can head to a hot springs on this 1-mile round trip trail. The Lightfeather Hot Springs boasts an average temperate of 130 F. Don't go into the springs, though – it contains an amoeba that causes a potentially fatal form of meningitis. The hikes includes two river crossings in which the water is about 2 feet deep. From the Gila Visitor Center parking lot, take the trail heading along the Middle Fork Gila River.

• **Trail #160** – A ridge overlooking the West Fork of the Gila River and Little Creek awaits on this 6.5-mile round trip. The trail gains 970 feet in elevation. Start at the Woody's Corral Trailhead, about a mile from the visitor center on the road to the cliff dwellings.

• **Little Bear Canyon Trail (aka Trail #729)** – Hikers can walk through an otherworldly spring-fed slot canyon carved out by the Middle Fork Gila River on this 8.5-mile round trip hike. Be aware that only the final 0.44 miles of the hike is in the slot canyon. Start at the TJ Corral Trailhead, which is about a mile from the visitor center on the road to the cliff dwellings.

• **Trail to the Past** – The ruins of a single ancient Puebloan dwelling sit at the head of a canyon on this 0.5-mile round trip trail. The trail also passes a large pictograph panel along the river. The trailhead is next to the Lower Scorpion Campground.

• **West Fork Trail** – For a short but scenic walk, try this 0.34-mile round trip walk along the pretty west fork of the Gila River. The trailhead is next to the Cliff Dwellings parking lot and can be done in conjunction with a hike to the ancient complex.

Chiracahua National Monument
Heart of Rocks Trail

Day hikers can enjoy a vast garden of hoodoos, most standing hundreds of feet in the air, on a remote trail at Arizona's Chiricahua National Monument.

The 7.6-mile round trip to the Heart of Rocks is not for the out of shape, as it includes some steep elevation gains in a dry, rocky region. The views and sights are worth getting physically fit for, though.

To reach the trailhead, from Wilcox, Ariz., take Ariz. Hwy. 186 southeast. Turn left/east onto Ariz. Hwy. 181. When the highway enters the national monument, it becomes E. Bonita Canyon Road. Park at the Chiricahua National Monument Visitor Center; if you've started traveling north and are on Scenic Drive, you've gone too far.

Take the Lower Rhyolite Canyon Trail, which leaves from the parking lot's east side. You're at 5400 feet elevation.

Intermittent Bonita Creek sits on trail's left/north side, as you hike up Rhyolite Canyon. On that side of the canyon also are rows and rows of hoodoos, and though they're a fantastic sight, this is just the salad before the main course.

Thanks to the creek and the higher elevation, the walk will be far greener than the desert you drove in on. The trail is a gradual ascent through the canyon, but the dirt path – constructed by the Civilian Conservation Corps in 1934 – is easy to walk.

At 1.5 miles, go left-straight/southeast on the Sarah Deming Trail. The elevation is 5980 feet.

As with Rhyolite Canyon, an intermittent creek runs on the trail's left/north. Sarah Deming Canyon is narrower, however, and more forested. In addition, springs on the canyon's sides generate trickles running a hundred feet or so into the creek.

Big Balanced Rock rises high above the Heart of Rocks Trail. A thousand-ton stone "sits" atop a 5-foot in diameter rock.

Another highlight are two chimney-shaped rocks.

After passing those rocks, the trail at roughly 2.7 miles veers left/north, crosses the creek, and leaves the canyon for the ridgetop. It will be a strenuous climb up. Fortunately, steps have been carved into the rock to make the trip easier.

At 3.1 miles, you'll reach the Big Balanced Rock Trail. The junction sits at 6860 feet. Go right/east onto the trail, treating it as a spur to Big Balanced Rock, which is just 0.1 miles away.

Big Balanced Rock is an impressive sight. It stands 25 feet tall, is 22 feet in diameter, and weighs 1,000 tons. The small section that the rock is "balanced" on is only 5 feet across.

After taking in the sight, head left/west on trail. At 3.3 miles, you'll arrive back at the junction with the Sarah Deming Trail. Go right/northeast; you're now on the stem trail for the Heart of Rocks Loop.

At 3.4 miles, the loop begins. Go left/west, taking loop clockwise, for the best views.

Several great sights await in the loop. Most are classic hoodoos – like Pinnacle Balanced Rock – but several form interesting shapes that merit names such as Old Maid, Camel's Head, Thor's Hammer, Punch and Judy (on the loop's north side), Duck on a Rock (loop's east side), and Kissing Rocks. There's also a narrow squeeze between two immense rocks and a view at the top of a rise that looks across hundreds of spires. Lichen covers many of the rocks, adding to their coloration and charm.

At 4.4 miles, you've completed the loop. Go left/south onto the stem trail.

The rhyolite pinnacles are here because of a volcanic eruption 27 million years ago at the Turkey Creek Caldera just south of the park.

At 4.5 miles, you come to the junction with the Sarah Deming Trail and the Big Balanced Rock Trail. Continue right/ southwest on Sarah Deming.

The volcanic eruptions threw ash and molten debris high into the air. Much of it settled and compacted at what is now the national monument, creating layers of rhyolite tuff that ran hundreds of feet deep.

The route reaches the junction with Lower Rhyolite Canyon Trail at 6.1 miles. Go left/west on it.

Rain easily broke through cracks in the weak tuff, causing it to fissure and crack and, with the help of wind, to erode over time. The result are the hoodoos seen in Heart of Rocks and throughout the park.

At 7.6 miles, the trail arrives at the visitor center' sparking lot.

Be sure to start any hike early in the day, especially if walking in spring or autumn, as the trail will get hot by mid-morning. Always carry water with you on this desert trail.

Other Chiracahua National Monument Trails

Though most visiting Chiricahua National Monument want to see the spectacular Heart of the Rocks, there are other great trails delivering impressive sights. Some lead to grand vistas while others head through verdant canyons. Some traverse montane forests while others offer the chance to see fascinating birds.

Bonita Canyon Road is the national monument's only road, so all trailheads are on it or a short spur off it. The trails listed here are arranged from west to east in the order they appear on the road:

• **Silver Spur Faraway Trail** – A pleasant walk through the high desert awaits on this 0.84-mile round trip. The trail starts on opposite of the road from the visitor center and ends at

BEST SIGHTS TO SEE AT WHITE SANDS NP   71

Bonita Canyon Campground. It actually is meant as a spur to the Faraway Trail, which runs west to the road of the same name. A side trail also meanders up Madrone Canyon to Silver Spur Trail.

• **Rhyolite Canyon Trail** – This 4.8-mile round trip hike heads through a fairly verdant canyon. It often is used as an access route to the Heart of Rocks region. Start at the far end of the visitor center parking lot and turn back upon coming to the trail leading into Sarah Deming Canyon.

• **Natural Bridge Trail** – The 4-mile round trip heads through oak and juniper woodlands to the top of one canyon and into another one that sports an Apache pine forest. An arch is visible at trail's end from across the canyon. Parking is along the road's side.

• **Sugar Mountain Trail** – The hike heads 1.8 miles round trip to the top of Suglarloaf Mountain, which at 7310 feet is one of the highest points in the area. Since you're already at a high elevation, the trail only needs to gain 482 feet in elevation. At the summit are 360 degree views and a fire tower. Turn right/ west onto the road leading to the Echo Canyon Trailhead; pass it and continue to the spur road's end.

• **Echo Canyon Trail** – The 2.8-miles round trip hike passes impressive rock formations. If a birder, visit in summer when white-throated swifts are common. Turn back at the junction with the Hailstone Trail or continue on it and connect with the Ed Riggs Trail for a loop back to the trailhead. Park by turning right/west onto the spur road leading to the Echo Canyon Trailhead.

• **Ed Riggs Trail** – Hikers can ramble through a sparse forest past rock spires on this 1.4-mile round trip. The trail begins at the Echo Canyon Trailhead; start on Echo Canyon Trail then when the route splits, go left/northeast. Turn back at that junction with Mushroom Rock Trail, which leads to the Heart of the Rocks area.

• **Massai Point Trail** – The trails runs a half-mile around the 6884 foot summit at the end of Bonita Canyon Road where it loops back upon itself. A mere 49 feet in elevation is gained on the trail. The north section is concrete sidewalk and wheel-chair accessible.

Saguaro National Park
Deer Valley Loop

Day hikers can walk through a forest of saguaro cactus on the Deer Valley Loop near Tucson.

The roughly 3.5 mile route at Saguaro National Park (East) consists of several connecting trails. As a number of trails criss-cross this area, the route easily can be shortened or lengthened. The loop described here, however, tends to give the most scenic views.

The best season to hike the loop is March through May when temperatures are pleasant. Summer will be unbearably hot and winter potentially cool. Many desert plants also bloom in April and May, making for a colorful landscape.

To reach the trailhead, from the junction of Interstate 10 and Speedway Boulevard in Tucson, take the latter east. This heads to the north side of Saguaro National Park East. Park in the pullout at the Wildhorse Trailhead on the road's right/south side.

Begin the loop by heading southwest on Wild Horse Canyon Trail. You'll pass the Shantz Trail on the right, an unnamed connector on the left, then the Creosote Trail on the right.

Close to the road, you'll see small saguaro cactus still shorter than the shrubs they grow amid. The farther from the road you walk, though, and the saguaro quickly become much taller and are all around you.

An icon of the American West, these lords of the desert can grow up to 50 feet high and weigh several tons. With so little rainfall, decades are needed for the saguaro to reach its dominating size.

As approaching the Bajada Wash, a cool saguaro cactus to look for is one that's crested. Only about 1 in 10,000 saguaros are crested, biologists estimate. Near that sight, the Bajada

Wash Trail comes in from the right and then after a bit departs to the left.

Saguaro cacti begin their lives by sprouting under small trees, such as the little leaf palo verde, growing only about an inch a year. They soon dwarf the tree – and with taproots that reach a yard deep and almost 30 years in diameter – kill the very tree that sheltered them.

At 1 mile, the route reaches Garwood Trail. Go right/south onto it. You'll gradually head uphill.

The giant saguaro sometimes blooms only once every 35 years, so they must live an extremely long time for the species to survive. The typical saguaro stays on the earth for 150 years, but some at the national park are more than 200 years old.

Upon reaching the 1.5 mile mark, go right/west onto the Carrillo Trail. This will take you to a ridge overlooking a wash. Great views of Rincon Mountains to the southeast are to be had.

If hoping to visit when saguaro's pretty white flowers bloom, plan your hike for April through June. The flower opens during the night and closes in midafternoon.

At 1.8 miles, the route comes to Deer Valley Trail. Go right/ north onto it and continue downhill.

The saguaro's primary pollinators are honey bees, bats, and white-winged doves, but a variety of songbirds help as well. Pollination leads to ruby red fruits that ripen in June. Though each fruit has around 2000 seeds, only about 1 percent of them will germinate.

At 2.2 miles, the route reaches the descent's bottom, where the Squeeze Pen Trail awaits. Take it right/northeast.

Several animals rely on the saguaro cactus not just for nour- ishment but as their home. The saguaro's sharp, regularly spaced thorns provide perfect protection for nests. Gila wood-

The Deer Valley Loop heads through a saguaro cactus forest on a series of connecting trails.

peckers and gilded flickers will cut holes into the saguaro and upon moving out, other birds become squatters.

This leg of the trail passes the Bajada Vista Trail on the right. At 2.7 miles is the Vanover Trail junction; at it, continue straight-right/north onto the Kennedy Trail.

In addition to songbirds using saguaros, during any hike of this loop you're certain to see harmless small lizards darting about. Horse riders often use the equestrian trails, giving you a feel of being in the Old West.

At 3.1 miles, the route arrives at the Shantz Trail junction. Turn right/northeast onto it and head back to the Wild Horse Canyon Trail, where you'll go left/north to the trailhead.

There's absolutely no shade along the loop, so be sure to don sunscreen, sunglasses and sunhat. In addition, if caught in a storm do not stand near the saguaro, as it's a natural lightning rod, having absorbed salt from the desert floor.

Other Saguaro National Park Trails

Among the best ways to see Saguaro National Park's top sights is via a day hike. Just five short trails will allow you to enjoy each of the park's highlights – towering saguaros, desert wildflowers, petroglyphs, the Javelina Rocks, and Sonoran Desert wildlife.

Saguaros

One of the park's densest populations of saguaro cactus grows along the **Valley View Overlook Trail** in the park's Tucson Mountain District (Saguaro Park West). The 0.8-mile round trip trail is flat and can easily be traversed by children. Its trailhead is off of Bajada Loop Drive.

Desert wildflowers

Though many think of deserts as barren and inhospitable, they bloom in a glorious array of colors each spring following a rainfall. Among the best hikes for seeing Sonoran Desert flowers – cholla, prickly pear and barrel cactus – with mountain ranges lining the horizon is the 1.3-mile **Freeman Homestead Trail** at the Javelina Picnic Area (Saguaro Park East).

Petroglyphs

Hohokam petroglyphs of spirals, circles and a variety of other geometric shapes were created by Native American groups that resided in the desert between 500-1100 A.D. You can see hundreds of them is the 0.4-mile round trip **Signal Hill Trail** in the park's Tucson Mountain District (Saguaro Park West).

Javelina Rocks

Among the most popular picnic spots in the national park is the Javelina Rocks, located off of Cactus Forest Drive (Saguaro

The roadrunner is among Saguaro National Park's many denizens.

Park East). Formed more than 25 million years ago, the rocks are an interesting example of Catalina Gneiss, in which sheets of other minerals were melted into one another while deep underground. The oft-photographed rocks also mark the trailhead for the **Tanque Verde Ridge Trail**, a 6.9-mile one-way route that offers some excellent views of the Tucson basin.

Desert wildlife

Coyotes, roadrunners, jackrabbits and quail all thrive in the Sonoran Desert that stretches across Arizona and northern Mexico. Many of these creatures – or at least signs of them – can be seen on the 6.05-mile (one-way) **Douglas Spring Trail** in the Rincon Mountain District (Saguaro Park East).

Hiking is a fantastic family activity, but to avoid disasters, always plan ahead and have the right gear.

Bonus Section I: Day Hiking Primer

Y ou'll get more out of a day hike if you research it and plan ahead. It's not enough to just pull over to the side of the road and hit a trail that you've never been on and have no idea where it goes. In fact, doing so invites disaster.

Instead, you should preselect a trail (This book's trail descriptions can help you do that). You'll also want to ensure that you have the proper clothing, equipment, navigational tools, first-aid kit, food and water. Knowing the rules of the trail and potential dangers along the way also are helpful. In this special section, we'll look at each of these topics to ensure you're fully prepared.

Selecting a Trail

For your first few hikes, stick to short, well-known trails where you're likely to encounter others. Once you get a feel for hiking, your abilities, and your interests, expand to longer and more remote trails.

Always check to see what the weather will be like on the trail you plan to hike. While an adult might be able to withstand wind and a sprinkle here or there, for kids it can be pure misery. Dry, pleasantly warm days with limited wind always are best when hiking with children.

Don't choose a trail that is any longer than the least fit person in your group can hike. Adults in good shape can go 8-

12 miles a day; for kids, it's much less. There's no magical number.

When planning the hike, try to find a trail with a mid-point payoff – that is something you and definitely any children will find exciting about half-way through the hike. This will help keep up everyone's energy and enthusiasm during the journey.

If you have children in your hiking party, consider a couple of additional points when selecting a trail.

Until children enter their late teens, they need to stick to trails rather than going off-trail hiking, which is known as bushwhacking. Children too easily can get lost when off trail. They also can easily get scratched and cut up or stumble across poisonous plants and dangerous animals.

Generally, kids will prefer a circular route to one that requires hiking back the way you came. The return trip often feels anti-climatic, but you can overcome that by mentioning features that all of you might want to take a closer look at.

Once you select a trail, it's time to plan for your day hike. Doing so will save you a lot of grief – and potentially prevent an emergency. You are, after all, entering the wilds, a place where help may not be readily available.

When planning your hike, follow these steps:
• Print a road map showing how to reach the parking lot near the trailhead. Outline the route with a transparent yellow highlighter and write out the directions.
• Print a satellite photo of the parking area and the trailhead. Mark the trailhead on the photo.
• Print a topo map of the trail. Outline the trail with the yellow highlighter. Note interesting features you want to see along the trail and the destination.
• If carrying GPS, program this information into your device.
• Make a timeline for your trip, listing: when you will leave

home; when you will arrive at the trailhead; your turn back time; when you will return for home in your vehicle; and when you will arrive at your home.

• Estimate how much water and food you will need to bring based on the amount of time you plan to spend on the trail and in your vehicle. You'll need at least two pints of water per person for every hour on the trail.

• Fill out two copies of a hiker's safety form. Leave one in your vehicle.

• Share all of this information with a responsible person remaining in civilization, leaving a hiker's safety form with them. If they do not hear from you within an hour of when you plan to leave the trail in your vehicle, they should contact authorities to report you as possibly lost.

Clothing
Footwear

If your feet hurt, the hike is over, so getting the right footwear is worth the time. Making sure the footwear fits before hitting the trail also is a good idea. With children, if you've gone a few weeks without hiking, that's plenty of time for feet to grow, and they may have just outgrown their hiking boots. Check out everyone's footwear a few days before heading out on the hike. If it doesn't fit, replace it.

For flat, smooth, dry trails, sneakers and cross-trainers are fine, but if you really want to head onto less traveled roads or tackle areas that aren't typically dry, you'll need hiking boots. Once you start doing any rocky or steep trails – and remember that a trail you consider moderately steep needs to be only half that angle for a child to consider it extremely steep – you'll want hiking boots, which offer rugged tread perfect for handling rough trails.

Socks

Socks serve two purposes: to wick sweat away from skin and to provide cushioning. Cotton socks aren't very good for hiking, except in extremely dry environments, because they retain moisture that can lead to blisters. Wool socks or liner socks work best. You'll want to look for three-season socks, also known as trekking socks. While a little thicker than summer socks, their extra cushioning generally prevents blisters. Also, make sure kids don't put on holey socks; that's just inviting blisters.

Layering

On all but hot, dry days, when hiking you should wear multiple layers of clothing that provide various levels of protection against sweat, heat loss, wind and potentially rain. Layering works because the type of clothing you select for each stratum serves a different function, such as wicking moisture or shielding against wind. In addition, trapped air between each layer of clothing is warmed by your body heat. Layers also can be added or taken off as needed.

Generally, you need three layers. Closest to your skin is the wicking layer, which pulls perspiration away from the body and into the next layer, where it evaporates. Exertion from walking means you will sweat and generate heat, even if the weather is cold. The second layer provides insulation, which helps keep you warm. The last layer is a water-resistant shell that protects you from rain, wind, snow and sleet.

As the seasons and weather change, so does the type of clothing you select for each layer. The first layer ought to be a loose-fitting T-shirt in summer, but in winter and on other cold days you might opt for a long-sleeved moisture-wicking synthetic material, like polypropylene. During winter, the next layer probably also should cover the neck, which often is exposed to the elements. A turtleneck works fine, but preferably not one made of cotton. The third layer in winter, depending on the temperature, could be a wool sweater, a half-zippered long sleeved fleece jacket, or a fleece vest. You might even add a fourth layer of a hooded parka with pockets, made of material that can block wind and resist water. Gloves or mittens as well as a hat also are necessary on cold days.

Headgear

Half of all body heat is lost through the head, hence the hiker's adage, "If your hands are cold, wear a hat." In cool, wet weather, wearing a hat is at least good for avoiding hypothermia, a potentially deadly condition in which heat loss occurs faster than the body can generate it. Children are more susceptible to hypothermia than adults.

Especially during summer, a hat with a wide brim is useful in keeping the sun out of eyes. It's also nice should rain start falling.

For young children, get a hat with a chin strap. They like to play with their hats, which will fly off in a wind gust if not fastened some way to the child.

Sunglasses

Sunglasses are an absolute must if walking through open areas exposed to the sun and in winter when you can suffer from snow blindness. Look for 100% UV-protective shades, which provide the best screen.

Equipment

A couple of principles should guide your purchases. First,

the longer and more complex the hike, the more equipment you'll need. Secondly, your general goal is to go light. Since you're on a day hike, the amount of gear you'll need is a fraction of what backpackers shown in magazines and catalogues usually carry. Still, the inclination of most day hikers is to not carry enough equipment. For the lightness issue, most gear today is made with titanium and siliconized nylon, ensuring it is sturdy yet fairly light. While the following list of what you need may look long, it won't weigh much.

Backpacks

Sometimes called daypacks (for day hikes or for kids), backpacks are essential to carry all of the essentials you need – snacks, first-aid kit, extra clothing.

For day hiking, you'll want to get an internal frame, in which the frame giving the backpack its shape is inside the pack's fabric so it's not exposed to nature. Such frames usually are lightweight and comfortable. External frames have the frame outside the pack, so they are exposed to the elements. They are excellent for long hikes into the backcountry when you must carry heavy loads.

As kids get older, and especially after they've been hiking for a couple of years, they'll want a "real" backpack. Unfortunately, most backpacks for kids are overbuilt and too heavy. Even light ones that safely can hold up to 50 pounds are inane for most children.

When buying a daypack for your child, look for sternum straps, which help keep the strap on the shoulders. This is vital for prepubescent children, as they do not have the broad shoulders that come with adolescence, meaning packs likely will slip off and onto their arms, making them uncomfortable and difficult to carry. Don't buy a backpack that a child will "grow into." Backpacks that don't fit well simply will lead to sore shoulder and back muscles and could result in poor posture.

Also, consider purchasing a daypack with a hydration system for kids. This will help ensure they drink a lot of water. More on this later when we get to canteens.

Before hitting the trail, always check your children's backpacks to make sure that they have not overloaded them. Kids think they need more than they really do. They also tend to overestimate their own ability to carry stuff. Sibling rivalries often lead to children packing more than they should in their rucksacks, too. Don't let them overpack "to teach them a lesson," though, as it can damage bones and turn the hike into a bad experience.

A good rule of thumb is no more than 25 percent capacity. Most upper elementary school kids can carry only about 10 pounds for any short distance. Subtract the weight of the backpack, and that means only 4-5 pounds in the backpack. Overweight children will need to carry a little less than this or they'll quickly be out of breath.

Child carriers

You'll have to carry infant and toddlers. Until infants can hold their heads up, which usually doesn't happen until about four to six months of age, a front pack (like a Snugli or Baby Bjorn) is best. It keeps the infant close for warmth and balances out your backpack. At the same time, though, you must watch for baby overheating in a front pack, so you'll need to remove the infant from your body at rest stops.

Once children reach about 20 pounds, they typically can hold their heads up and sit on their own. At that point, you'll want a baby carrier (sometimes called a child carrier or baby backpack), which can transfer the infant's weight to your hips when you walk. You'll not only be comfortable, but your child will love it, too.

Look for a baby carrier that is sturdy yet lightweight. Your child is going to get heavier as time passes, so about the only way you can counteract this is to reduce the weight of the items you use to carry things. The carrier also should have adjustment points, as you don't want your child to outgrow the carrier too soon. A padded waist belt and padded shoulder straps are necessary for your comfort. The carrier should provide some kind of head and neck support if you're hauling an infant. It also should offer back support for children of all ages, and leg holes should be wide enough so there's no chafing. You want to be able to load your infant without help, so it should be stable enough to stand that way when you take it off the child can sit in it for a moment while you get turned around. Stay away from baby carriers with only shoulder straps, as you need the waist belt to help shift the child's weight to your hips for more comfortable walking.

Fanny packs

Also known as a belt bag, a fanny pack is virtually a must for anyone with a baby carrier, as you can't otherwise lug a backpack. If your significant other is with you, he or she can carry the backpack, of course. Still, the fanny pack also is a good alternative to a backpack in hot weather, as it will reduce back sweat.

If you have only one or two kids on a hike, or if they also are old enough to carry daypacks, your fanny pack need not be large. A mid-size pouch can carry at least 200 cubic inches of supplies, which is more than enough to accommodate all the materials you need. A good fanny pack also has a spot for hooking canteens to.

Canteens

Canteens or plastic bottles filled with water are vital for any hike, no matter how short the trail. You'll need to have enough of them to carry about two pints of water per person for every hour of hiking.

Trekking poles

Also known as walking poles or walking sticks, trekking poles are necessary for maintaining stability on uneven or wet surfaces and to help reduce fatigue. The latter makes them useful on even surfaces. By transferring weight to the arms, a trekking pole can reduce stress on your knees and lower back, allowing you to maintain a better posture and to go farther.

If an adult with a baby or toddler on your back, you'll primarily want a trekking pole to help you maintain your balance, even if on a flat surface, and to help absorb some of the impact of your step.

Graphite tips provide the best traction. A basket just above the tip is a good idea so the stick doesn't sink into mud or sand. Angled cork handles are ergonomic and help absorb sweat from your hands so they don't blister. A strap on the handle to wrap around your hand is useful so the stick doesn't slip out. Telescopic poles are a good idea as you can adjust them as needed based on the terrain you're hiking and as kids grow to accommodate their height.

The pole also needs to be sturdy enough to handle rugged terrain, as you don't want a pole that bends when you press it to the ground. Spring-loaded shock absorbers help when heading down a steep incline but aren't necessary. Indeed, for a short walk across flat terrain, the right length stick is about all you need.

Carabiners
   Carabiners are metal loops, vaguely shaped like a D, with a sprung or screwed gate. You'll find that hooking a couple of them to your backpack or fanny pack useful in many ways. For example, if you need to dig through a fanny pack, you can hook the strap of your trekking pole to it. Your hat, camera straps, first-aid kit, and a number of other objects also can connect to them. Hook carabiners to your fanny pack or backpack upon purchasing them so you don't forget them when packing. Small carabiners with sprung gates are inexpensive, but they do have a limited life span of a couple of dozen hikes.

Navigational Tools
Paper maps
   Paper maps may sound passé in this age of GPS, but you'll find the variety and breadth of view they offer to be useful. During the planning process, a paper map (even if viewing it online), will be far superior to a GPS device. On the hike, you'll also want a backup to GPS. Or like many casual hikers, you may not own GPS at all, which makes paper maps indispensable.
   Standard road maps (which includes printed guides and handmade trail maps) show highways and locations of cities and parks. Maps included in guidebooks, printed guides handed out at parks, and those that are hand-drawn tend to be designed like road maps, and often carry the same positives and negatives.
   Topographical maps give contour lines and other important details for crossing a landscape. You'll find them invaluable on a hike into the wilds. The contour lines' shape and their spacing on a topo map show the form and steepness of a hill or

bluff, unlike the standard road map and most brochures and hand-drawn trail maps. You'll also know if you're in a woods, which is marked in green, or in a clearing, which is marked in white. If you get lost, figuring out where you are and how to get to where you need to be will be much easier with such information.

Aerial photos offer a view from above that is rendered exactly as it would look from an airplane. Thanks to Google and other online services, you can get fairly detailed pictures of the landscape. Such pictures are an excellent resource when researching a hiking trail. Unfortunately, those pictures don't label what a feature is or what it's called, as would a topo map. Unless there's a stream, determining if a feature is a valley bottom or a ridgeline also can be difficult. Like topo maps, satellite and aerial photos can be out of date a few years.

GPS

By using satellites, the global positioning system can find your spot on the Earth to within 10 feet. With a GPS device, you can preprogram the trailhead location and mark key turns and landmarks as well as the hike's end point. This mobile map is a powerful technological tool that almost certainly ensures you won't get lost – so long as you've correctly programmed the information. GPS also can calculate travel time and act as a compass, a barometer and altimeter, making such devices vir-tually obsolete on a hike.

In remote areas, however, reception is spotty at best for GPS, rendering your mobile map worthless. A GPS device also runs on batteries, and there's always a chance they will go dead. Or you may drop your device, breaking it in the process. Their screens are small, and sometimes you need a large paper map to get a good sense of the natural landmarks around you.

Compass

Like a paper map, a compass is indispensable even if you use GPS. Should your GPS no longer function, the compass then can be used to tell you which direction you're heading. A protractor compass is best for hiking. Beneath the compass needle is a transparent base with lines to help your orient yourself. The compass often serves as a magnifying glass to help you make out map details. Most protractor compasses also come with a lanyard for easy carrying.

Food and Water

Water

As water is the heaviest item you'll probably carry, there is a temptation to not take as much as one should. Don't skimp on the amount of water you bring, though; after all, it's the one supply your body most needs. It's always better to end up having more water than needed than returning to your vehicle dehydrated.

How much water should you take? Adults need at least a quart for every two hours hiking. Children need to drink about a quart every two hours of walking and more if the weather is hot or dry. To keep kids hydrated, have them drink at every rest stop.

Don't presume there will be drinking water on the hiking trail. Most trails outside of urban areas lack such an amenity. In addition, don't drink water from local streams, lakes, rivers or ponds. There's no way to tell if local water is safe or not. As soon as you have consumed half of your water supply, you should turn around for the vehicle.

Food

Among the many wonderful things about hiking is that

snacking between meals isn't frowned upon. Unless going on an all-day hike in which you'll picnic along the way, you want to keep everyone in your hiking party fed, especially as hunger can lead to lethargic and discontented children. It'll also keep young kids from snacking on the local flora or dirt. Before hitting the trail, you'll want to repackage as much of the food as possible as products sold at grocery stores tend to come in bulky packages that take up space and add a little weight to your backpack. Place the food in re-sealable plastic bags.

Bring a variety of small snacks for rest stops. You don't want kids filling up on snacks, but you do need them to maintain their energy levels if they're walking or to ensure they don't turn fussy if riding in a child carrier. Go for complex carbohydrates and proteins for maintaining energy. Good options include dried fruits, jerky, nuts, peanut butter, prepared energy bars, candy bars with a high protein content (nuts, peanut butter), crackers, raisins and trail mix (called "gorp"). A number of trail mix recipes are available online; you and your children may want to try them out at home to see which ones you collectively like most.

Salty treats rehydrate better than sweet treats do. Chocolate and other sweets are fine if they're not all that's served, but remember they also tend to lead to thirst and to make sticky messes. Whichever snacks you choose, don't experiment with food on the trail. Bring what you know kids will like.

Give the first snack within a half-hour of leaving the trailhead or you risk children becoming tired and whiny from low energy levels. If kids start asking for them every few steps even after having something to eat at the last rest stop, consider timing snacks to reaching a seeable landmark, such as, "We'll get out the trail mix when we reach that bend up ahead."

Milk for infants

If you have an infant or unweaned toddler with you, milk is as necessary as water. Children who only drink breastfed milk but don't have their mother on the hike require that you have breast-pumped milk in an insulated beverage container (such as a Thermos) that can keep it cool to avoid spoiling. Know how much the child drinks and at what frequency so you can bring enough. You'll also need to carry the child's bottle and feeding nipples. Bring enough extra water in your canteen so you can wash out the bottle after each feeding. A handkerchief can be used to dry bottles between feedings.

Don't forget the baby's pacifier. Make sure it has a string and hook attached so it connects to the baby's outfit and isn't lost.

What not to bring

Avoid soda and other caffeinated beverages, alcohol, and energy pills. The caffeine will dehydrate children as well as you. Alcohol has no place on the trail; you need your full faculties when making decisions and driving home. Energy pills essentially are a stimulant and like alcohol can lead to bad calls. If you're tired, get some sleep and hit the trail another day.

First-aid Kit

After water, this is the most essential item you can carry.

A first-aid kit should include:
- Adhesive bandages of various types and sizes, especially butterfly bandages (for younger kids, make sure they're colorful kid bandages)
- Aloe vera
- Anesthetic (such as Benzocaine)
- Antacid (tablets)

- Antibacterial (aka antibiotic) ointment (such as Neosporin or Bacitracin)
- Anti-diarrheal tablets (for adults only, as giving this to a child is controversial)
- Anti-itch cream or calamine lotion
- Antiseptics (such as hydrogen peroxide, iodine or Betadine, Mercuroclear, rubbing alcohol)
- Baking soda
- Breakable (or instant) ice packs
- Cotton swabs
- Disposable syringe (w/o needle)
- Epipen (if children or adults have allergies)
- Fingernail clippers (your multi-purpose tool might have this, and if so you can dispense with it)
- Gauze bandage
- Gauze compress pads (2x2 individually wrapped pad)
- Hand sanitizer (use this in place of soap)
- Liquid antihistamine (not Benadryl tablets, however, as children should take liquid not pills; be aware that liquid antihistamines may cause drowsiness)
- Medical tape
- Moisturizer containing an anti-inflammatory
- Mole skin
- Pain reliever (aka aspirin; for children's pain relief, use liquid acetaminophen such Tylenol or liquid ibuprofen; never give aspirin to a child under 12)
- Poison ivy cream (for treatment)
- Poison ivy soap
- Powdered sports drinks mix or electrolyte additives
- Sling
- Snakebite kit
- Thermometer

- Tweezers (your multi-purpose tool may have this allowing you to dispense with it)
- Water purification tablets

If infants are with you, be sure to also carry teething ointment (such as Orajel) and diaper rash treatment.

Many of the items should be taken out of their store packaging to make placement in your fanny pack or backpack easier. In addition, small amounts of some items – such as baking soda and cotton swabs – can be placed inside re-sealable plastic bags, since you won't need the whole amount purchased.

Make sure the first-aid items are in a waterproof container. A re-sealable plastic zipper bag is perfectly fine. As Indiana Dunes National Park sports a moist climate, be sure to re-place the adhesive bandages every couple of months, as they can deteriorate in the moistness. Also, check your first-aid kit every few trips and after any hike in which you've just used it, so that you can replace used components and to make sure medicines haven't expired.

If you have older elementary-age kids and teenagers who've been trained in first aid, giving them a kit to carry as well as yourself is a good idea. Should they find themselves lost or if you cannot get to them for a few moments, the kids might need to provide very basic first aid to one another.

Hiking with Children: Attitude Adjustment

To enjoy hiking with kids, you'll first have to adopt your child's perspective. Simply put, we must learn to hike on our kids' schedules – even though they may not know that's what we're doing.

Compared to adults, kids can't walk as far, they can't walk as fast, and they will grow bored more quickly. Every step we take requires three for them. In addition, early walkers, up to two years of age, prefer to wander than to "hike." Preschool kids will start to walk the trail, but at a rate of only about a mile per hour. With stops, that can turn a three-mile hike into a four-hour journey. Kids also won't be able to hike as steep of trails as you or handle as inclement of weather as you might.

This all may sound limiting, especially to long-time backpackers used to racking up miles or bagging peaks on their hikes, but it's really not. While you may have to put off some backcountry and mountain climbing trips for a while, it also opens to you a number of great short trails and nature hikes with spectacular sights that you may have otherwise skipped because they weren't challenging enough.

So sure, you'll have to make some compromises, but the payout is high. You're not personally on the hike to get a workout but to spend quality time with your children.

Family Dog

Dogs are part of the family, and if you have children, they'll want to share the hiking experience with their pets. In turn, dogs will have a blast on the trail, some larger dogs can be used as Sherpas, and others will defend against threatening animals.

But there is a downside to dogs. Many will chase animals and so run the risk of getting lost or injured. Also, a doggy bag will have to be carried for dog pooh – yeah, it's natural, but also inconsiderate to leave for other hikers to smell and for their kids to step in. In addition, most dogs almost always will lose a battle against a threatening animal, so there's a price to be paid for your safety.

Many places where you'll hike solve the dilemma for you as dogs aren't allowed on their trails. Dogs are verboten on some state and national parks trails but usually permitted on those in national forests. Always check with the park ranger before heading to the trail.

If you can bring a dog, make sure it is well behaved and friendly to others. You don't need your dog biting another hiker while unnecessarily defending the family.

Rules of the Trail

Ah, the woods or a wide open meadow, peaceful and quiet, not a single soul around for miles. Now you and your children can do whatever you want.

Not so fast.

Act like wild animals on a hike, and you'll destroy the very aspects of the wilds that make them so attractive. You're also likely to end up back in civilization, specifically an emergency room. And there are other people around. Just as you would wish them to treat you courteously, so you and your children should do the same for them.

Let's cover how to act civilized on the trail.

Minimize damage to your surroundings

When on the trail, follow the maxim of "Leave no trace." Obviously, you shouldn't toss litter on the ground, start rock-slides, or pollute water supplies. How much is damage and how much is good-natured exploring is a gray area, of course. Most serious backpackers will say you should never pick up objects, break branches, throw rocks, pick flowers, and so on – the idea is not to disturb the environment at all.

Good luck getting a four-year-old to think like that. The good news is a four-year-old won't be able to throw around many rocks or break most branches.

Still, children from their first hike into the wilderness should be taught to respect nature and to not destroy their environment. While you might overlook a preschooler hurling rocks into a puddle, they can be taught to sniff rather than pick flowers. As they grow older, you can teach them the value of leaving the rock alone. Regardless of age, don't allow children to write on boulders or carve into trees.

Many hikers split over picking berries. To strictly abide by the "minimize damage" principle, you wouldn't pick any berries at all. Kids, however, are likely to find great pleasure in eating blackberries, currants and thimbleberries as ambling down the trail. Personally, I don't see any problem enjoying a few berries if the long-term payoff is a respect and love for nature. To minimize damage, teach them to only pick berries they can reach from the trail so they don't trample plants or deplete food supplies for animals. They also should only pick what they'll eat.

Collecting is another issue. In national and most state and county parks, taking rocks, flower blossoms and even pine cones is illegal. Picking flowers moves many species, especially if they are rare and native, one step closer to extinction. Archeological ruins are extremely fragile, and even touching them can damage a site.

But on many trails, especially gem trails, collecting is part of the adventure. Use common sense – if the point of the trail is to find materials to collect, such as a gem trail, take judiciously, meaning don't overcollect. Otherwise, leave it there.

Sometimes the trail crosses private land. If so, walking around fields, not through them, always is best or you could damage a farmer's crops.

Pack out what you pack in

Set the example as a parent: Don't litter yourself; whenever stopping, pick up whatever you've dropped; and always require kids to pick up after themselves when they litter. In the spirit of "Leave no trace," try to leave the trail cleaner than you found it, so if you come across litter that's safe to pick up, do so and bring it back to a trash bin in civilization. Given this, you may want to bring a plastic bag to carry out garbage.

Picking up litter doesn't just mean gum and candy wrappers but also some organic materials that take a long time to decompose and aren't likely to be part of the natural environment you're hiking. In particular, these include peanut shells, orange peelings, and eggshells.

Burying litter, by the way, isn't viable. Either animals or erosion soon will dig it up, leaving it scattered around the trail and woods.

Stay on the trail

Hiking off trail means potentially damaging fragile growth. Following this rule not only ensures you minimize damage but is also a matter of safety. Off trail is where kids most likely will encounter dangerous animals and poisonous plants. Not being able to see where they're stepping also increases the likelihood of falling and injuring themselves. Leaving the trail raises the chances of getting lost. Staying on the trail also means staying out of caves, mines or abandoned structures you may encounter. They are usually dangerous places.

Finally, never let children take a shortcut on a switchback trail. Besides putting them on steep ground upon which they could slip, their impatient act causes the switchback to erode.

Trail Dangers

While hikers generally are safe from animals on Joshua Tree National Park trails, sometimes a misstep or poor decision can lead to problems.

Snakes

Rattlesnakes live in the national park, but fortunately they are most active from April through October when the heat keeps hikers off the trail. In addition, poisonous snakes don't always inject venom when they bite, and some only spew a small amount that is survivable.

You can avoid snakes by staying out of desert scrub. Don't stick hands into dark holes and rocky crevices, don't turn over rocks, and don't hike at dusk or night when many snakes hunt. While climbing rocks, be careful where you stick your hand as a snake may be sunning itself.

If you see a snake, slowly back away from it. If you hear a rattle, stand still. In both cases, the snake usually will scoot off. Don't try to get a closer look, as it invites attack, especially from a rattler, because it then feels cornered. A snake can strike at about a third of its body length, so you'll probably be just far enough away that it won't strike. Also, don't mess with baby snakes for they too will bite.

Sometimes hikers walking through desert scrub don't even realize they've been bitten (this is why staying on the clear trail is vital), and sometimes you stumble a little too close to a snake. Bite symptoms include pain and burning at the bite site followed by swelling and blistering. Nausea and vomiting, with numbness and tingling about the mouth, fingers and scalp also are indications. If the bite is severe, the victim also will grow faint and dizzy and have a weak pulse and cold, clammy skin. They may go into shock.

To treat a snake bite, lay down and control your panic. Place a compression bandage lightly above the bite, as this can slow the spread of venom. Do not use a tourniquet, however. Then call for help and seek medical attention immediately.

Finally, if at all possible try to identify the snake so the right anti-venom can be used when the victim receives medical treatment.

Scorpions

Scorpions native to the national park generally are on the weak side where venom is concerned, and their sting often doesn't hurt more than a bee's.

You can avoid a scorpion sting by keeping your hands out of holes and crevices as well as by not overturning rocks, all of which could be homes for these little arthropods.

If stung, you'll feel instant pain or burning, numbness and tingling, and the bitten area will be sensitive to touch.

Treatment includes washing the stung area with soap and water then applying a cold compress to it. You also should elevate a stung limb above heart level. Always bring a young child stung by a scorpion to the emergency room. For older teens, if reactions in addition to those previously listed appear, bring them as well to the ER.

Spiders

The national park is home to the black widow and the tarantula. At worse, these spiders' bites will cause an allergic reaction, though they can be painful.

Unfortunately, most hikers don't know they've even been bit by spiders, as it often feels like a pinprick. As with mosquitoes, the reaction to a most spider bite is mostly just a nuisance.

If you feel an immediate burning, pain, redness and swelling, especially around a double fang mark, you probably are the victim of a black widow and should seek immediate medical attention.

To avoid spider bites, don't stick hands into dark holes, burrows or rocky crevices and don't turn over rocks. Spiders live in such areas and may bite if surprised and think they're under attack.

Treat a spider bite by washing the bite area with soap and water. A cold compress can help alleviate the swelling and redness. Diphenhydramine tablets can be taken to reduce the itch while acetaminophen will help relieve severe pain. If a severe reaction occurs or you know the bite was from a poisonous spider, seek immediate medical treatment.

A few don'ts ... Aspirin won't reduce the inflammation of a spider bite and shouldn't be taken by children. Don't bother with antibiotics, as they're not designed for treating spider bites. Finally, don't cut open the bite mark, as it may lead to infection.

For more about these topics and many others, pick up this author's "Hikes with Tykes: A Practical Guide to Day Hiking with Kids." You also can find tips online at the author's "Day Hiking Trails" blog. Have fun on the trail!

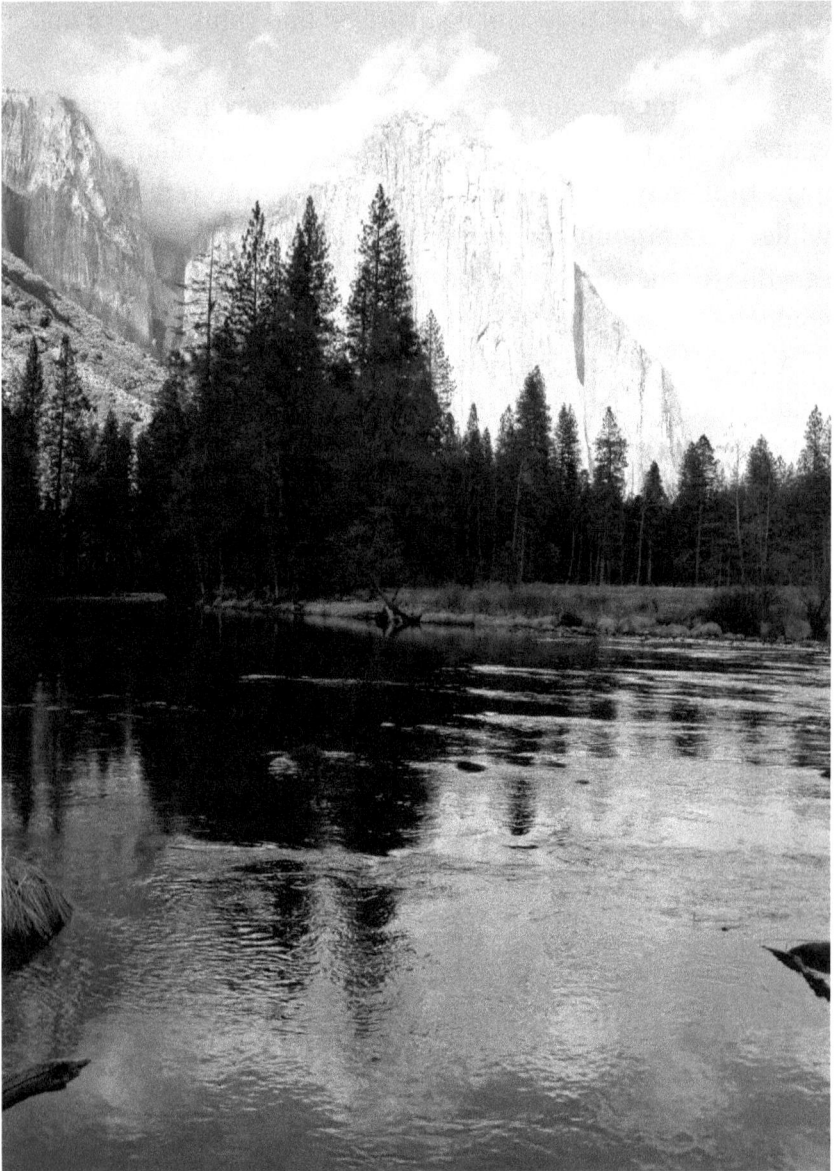

America's national parks preserve the nation's most impressive natural sights, such as El Capitan in Yosemite Valley at Yosemite National Park.

Bonus Section II: National Parks Primer

T he breadth of wonders at America's national parks astounds the mind. You can stand at the nation's rooftop with 60 peaks taller than 12,000 feet at Rocky Mountain National Park or in a gash in the earth more than a mile deep at Grand Canyon. You can visit among the driest places in the world where little more than an inch of rain falls per year upon the beige sands of Death Valley or step into the blue ocean itself at Biscayne National Park where the bulk of the wilderness is the Atlantic and its vibrantly colored coral reefs. You can see some of the oldest rock on Earth, like the 1.2 billion year-old granite at Shenandoah National Park, to some of the newest land on the planet at Hawai'i Volcanoes National Park where you can watch lava flows create new ground inch by inch before you. You can enjoy parks that are primarily historical and even urban in nature, such as Cuyahoga Valley National Park, which features pioneer farms and bicycle paths, while others preserve breathless, awe-inspiring tracts of wild-erness and stone, such as Yosemite's El Capitan and Half Dome. You can trek through caves with rooms larger than a football field hundreds of feet below the ground, such as at Carlsbad Caverns, or beneath trees soaring 15 stories over your head at Redwood National Park.

Given these grand wonders, not surprisingly national parks are a major travel destination. Indeed, many parks report record attendance during past few years. In 2018, annual attendance at parks operated by the National Parks Service hit an amazing 338 million visits – the highest level ever in more than a century of record-keeping.

But with so many sights and given most national parks' distance from major population centers, how can visitors be sure they'll make the best use of their time and see all of the highlights?

Unfortunately, many park visitors treat a national park like a drive-through restaurant. Fully experiencing any national park, though, requires that you "get out of the car." As W.H. Davies once wrote, "Now shall I walk/Or shall I ride?/'Ride,' Pleasure said; 'Walk,' Joy replied." A day hike can deliver the joy that each park offers.

What is (and isn't) a National Park

Often local tourism agencies and business groups will refer to the "national park" near their community. If you've done any amount of traveling, such statements on websites and brochures would lead you to believe that there are hundreds of national parks!

The truth of that matter is that many of those agencies and hometown boosters actually are referring to units administered by the National Park Service. The park service oversees more than 400 units, of which only 61 are actual national parks.

The types of units the park service manages are broken into more than 20 categories. Among the more common ones are national historical parks, national historic sites, national monuments, national memorials, national military parks, national battlefield parks, national battlefield sites, national battlefields, national preserves, and national reserves.

Other agencies also run parklands set aside for public use. The U.S. Forest Service overseas national forests. States and counties typically manage what are smaller versions of national parks and national forests. The U.S. Fish and Wildlife Service handles wildlife refuges while the Bureau of Land Management is in charge of wilderness areas.

As national forests and state parks adjoin national parks, travelers may not know when they've entered one unit or left another. Sometimes these different units even are operated as a single park, as is the case with the array of public lands protecting redwoods in northwestern California, to save costs.

National parks generally are considered the crown jewels of the park service's outdoor experiences. When visiting a national park, though, don't discount the surrounding state parks, national forests, and other recreational areas, as they also offer excellent sights to see. They're also often less crowded than a national park.

Choosing a Park to Visit

Planning a trip to a national park isn't like going to the mall. Unless you're lucky enough to live near a national park, any trip to one will be part of a vacation for you and your family. So you'll need to choose which park you want to visit.

Your interests

Begin by asking what you'd most like to see. Do you want to watch wildlife? Experience great geological features like canyons and exotic rock formations? Of deserts, volcanoes, autumn leaves, or tropical rain forests, which most appeals to you? Are you interested in history? Was there a park you've always wanted to visit since childhood?

The quandary you'll face is that you'll want to see more than you probably have vacation time for!

Getting there

Next, decide how you'll reach the park. Many parks are remote and require driving, at least from a nearby airport. How much time you have to travel and how much money you're able to spend on transportation can help you narrow your list of potential parks to visit during a vacation.

Costs

After that, determine how much money is in your budget. The good news is that the park itself is fairly inexpensive to visit. As of press time, Congaree National Park in South Carolina and Cuyahoga Valley National Park in Ohio are absolutely free to enter while at the upper end Grand Canyon National Park charges $30 a vehicle for a week-long stay.

Sometimes fees are reduced (and even waived) for students and military personnel. Generally, the vehicle pass you purchase is good for a few days.

Many times a year, the park service offers "free entrance days." Expect the park to be crowded on those days, however, as they often coincide with holidays.

If you plan to hike national parks regularly, you should consider purchasing a National Parks and Federal Recreational Lands Pass, which will get a noncommercial vehicle plus passholder and three passengers into any national park for less than $100 a year.

Even less expensive versions of the pass are available for senior citizens, the disabled and National Park volunteers. If you visit a number of parks over several weeks, you'll definitely save on admission costs going this route.

Be forewarned that there may be additional fees if planning

to camp or to park an RV. Almost any hike that involves being part of a tour group at a major destination within a park carries a cost beyond the entry fee.

The real cost will come in lodging and food. Hotels within national parks generally are pricey while those near the park entrances only slight less so. Camping in the park or a neighboring national forest can be a good, inexpensive option. Food also can cost a small fortune within a park, but usually there are plenty of good, less expensive alternatives in nearby communities.

When to visit

Another consideration is when you will travel. Parts of some parks, such as Rocky Mountain, Crater Lake and Yosemite, actually cannot be reached during winter as heavy snowfall closes high mountain roads. Others, such as Death Valley, are simply too dangerous to hike in the summer heat. Most parks also have a peak season in which roads, campgrounds, sites and trails will be crowded; visiting a park when attendance is low, but the weather good is ideal.

The high season typically is summer, running from Memorial Day through Labor Day weekends; those three-day weekends as well as when the Fourth of July falls on a Friday or Monday, usually draw the largest crowds in a year. In hot desert areas, the high season shifts slightly, as Death Valley and Arches national parks pull more people in late spring and early autumn when temperatures are pleasant.

The ideal time to visit is the off-season just before or just after high season. This can be difficult as usually high season coincides with when children are on school vacation.

Also think about the day of the week you will visit. You usually can avoid crowds by visiting weekdays, especially Monday through Thursday, when attendance dips. On three-day holiday weekends, sometimes the adjoining Thursday or Tuesday can see an uptick as well.

The time of day also plays a role. The earlier in the morning you can get to a national park, the less congested it will be on roadways and at popular sites. Usually, park visitors make their way from the nearest hotels mid-morning to the front gates and then set off again before sunset to their lodging. Note that visitor centers at some parks will close for holidays, usually Christmas.

Of course, visiting during the off-season and on weekdays comes with trade-offs. The weather may be cold or extremely hot; sometimes ranger-led park programs are nil on weekdays, especially in the off-season. In addition, access to some parks can be limited depending on the season. Yellowstone, for example, closes some of its entrances during winter as snowfall at the high elevations makes roads impassable. Other parks, such as Crater Lake, can't be reached at all during the off-season because of heavy snow.

Another possibility for avoiding crowds is to visit national parks that see low attendance overall. Yosemite, Yellowstone, the Grand Canyon and Cuyahoga national parks typically boast the highest attendance so definitely will be crowded during the high seasons. Great Basin (in Nevada) and Theodore Roosevelt (in North Dakota) national parks, however, are easy to reach but see few visitors compared to those in California, Arizona and Utah.

Pets

Pets are an important member of many families, and a vacation with them at a national park is possible, albeit with limitations.

Dogs and cats typically are only allowed in the park's developed areas, such as drive-in campgrounds and picnic areas, but rarely on trails. They also must be on a leash as well.

So if heading on a day hike, what to do with Rover or Queenie? Some parks offer kennels; short of that, one of your party will have to stay behind with the pet.

National forests surrounding the national park usually have more lenient rules regarding pets, so if camping you may want to consider pitching a tent there instead, though an adult member of the party still will have to stay with the dogs while everyone else hikes the national park.

Getting Kids Involved

Children obviously can benefit from visiting these great outdoors treasures. A trip to a national park will give any child fond memories that will literally last a lifetime. During their visit, they will experience their natural joy of discovery, certainly by seeing and exploring the sights themselves or perhaps through a touch table in which they get to feel fossils or a rabbit pelt at a visitor center. The visit alone will encourage their appreciation for nature. Take them on a hike through these wild areas, and they receive the bonus of exercise in the fresh air.

The National Park Service offers a variety of great, interactive programs aimed at teaching kids about nature through fun and adventure. They often become the more memorable moments of a park visit for children, and a few even give cool souvenirs at the end.

Among the programs:

• **Junior Ranger** – Most parks now offer some version of this program, in which kids by filling out a self-guided booklet and sometimes performing volunteer work can earn a Junior

Ranger patch or pin among other goodies.

• **Ranger-led activities** – Park rangers often host family-friendly activities on the park's geology, wildlife, ecology, history and other topics. Some parks during the evening provide programs in which kids can sit about a campfire and learn about nature.

• **Star parties** – Several national parks, especially those that are remote, offer nighttime viewings of the sky with telescopes. Your kids never will see a sky so brilliantly lit with stars.

• **Touch programs** – Some parks provide kids the opportunity to meet live animals or to touch cool found objects, such as turtle shells, feathers and rocks. They usually are held at the park's nature or visitor center.

Kids' activities aren't limited to just inside the park, however. Before even leaving on your trip, have your children:

• **Check out the park's website** – Many of the websites list activities specific to their park that later can be played on the drive to the park or during hikes.

• **Meet Smokey Bear virtually** – Younger kids can learn about forest fires and nature at Smokey Bear's official website: *www.smokeybear.com/kids*

• **Visit Webrangers** – Get kids excited about your trip with a stop at the Webrangers website (*www.nps.gov/webrangers*). Kids can play more than 50 online games that allow them to explore various national parks.

Hiking National Parks Tips

Day hiking usually isn't as simple as throwing on one's tennis shoes and hitting the trail. While that may be fine at a small city park, doing so in a national park can invite disaster. Though day hiking hardly requires as much gear or planning as a backpacking trip, you still need to bring some equipment and to think ahead.

Following these 10 simple guidelines should ensure your day hike is problem-free:

• **Know where you're going** – Look at a map of the trail before heading out on it. Bring a paper map and compass with you on the trail and check both frequently as you walk.

• **Get the right footwear** – If your feet hurt, the hike is over. Good-fitting hiking boots almost always are a must on wilderness trails while cross-trainers probably are fine for paved surfaces; sandals almost always are a no-no.

• **Bring water** – You'll need about two pints of water per person for every hour of hiking and even more if in hot or dry climates. Leave soda and sugary fruit drinks at home; they are no replacement for water.

• **Layer your clothing** – Doing so allows you to remove and put back on clothing as needed to suit the weather. Make sure the layer next to the body wicks moisture away from the skin while the outer layer protects against wind and rain.

• **Carry a first-aid kit** – A small kit that allows you to bandage cuts and that contains some emergency equipment such as matches and a whistle will suffice for short hikes.

• **Don't overpack** – A lighter backpack always is better than one full of stuff you don't need. At the same time, don't skimp on the essentials.

• **Use a trekking pole** – Unless the surface you're on is absolutely level, you'll find a walking stick helps reduce fatigue. This is especially true if you're carrying a backpack.

• **Follow the rules of the trail** – Leave no trace by not littering ("Pack out what you pack in.") and by staying on the trail. Don't deface rocks or destroy signage.

• **Don't forget a snack** – Trail mix as well as jerky can help you maintain energy on the trail. It's also a good motivator for any children with you.

• **Enjoy the journey** – Reaching the destination is never as important as having a good time on the way there. If with children, play games, pause when something grabs their attention, and never turn the hike into a death march.

Services and amenities

Services and amenities at national parks can vary greatly depending on the number of visitors and the part of the park you're in. You almost always can expect to find a visitor center and campgrounds with bathrooms; that doesn't mean there will be a restaurant or a vending machine with snacks and water on site, however.

If hoping to stay in a park lodge or at a campground, quickly make reservations; the same goes for hotels, motels and campgrounds near the park. A safe bet to ensure that a reservation can be made is make them at least six months ahead and up to a year in advance at the most popular parks.

Most parks have at least some trails available for those with disabilities to traverse. Be aware, however, that these trails may not head to a park's top sights.

Best sights to see

Which national park trails offer the best vistas? Lead to awesome waterfalls? Let you see wildlife? To enjoy fall colors? Here are some lists of the best national park trails for those and many other specific interests.

Beaches

Come summertime, there's almost no better place to be than the beach. The warmth of the sun upon your face, the sound of waves splashing against the shore, the blue water stretching into the horizon...

Among the most beautiful beaches you can visit are those in national parks. Thousands of miles of shoreline around lakes and along oceans are protected in our parks, and just like the wildlife and rock formations you're apt to find in most of them, the beaches won't disappoint either.

Here are six must-see beaches at our national parks.

Ocean Path Trail, Acadia National Park: Cobble beaches and hard bedrock make up most of the shoreline for the Atlantic Ocean that surrounds the Maine park's many islands. A rare exception is the 4.4-miles round trip Ocean Path Trail that heads from a sand beach to sea cliffs.

Convoy Point, Biscayne National Park: This boardwalk trail is flat and easy, running along the Florida mangrove shore known as Convoy Point. You'll follow the blue-green waters of Biscayne Bay and be able to spot some small, mangrove-covered islands. Bring a lunch; there's a picnic area below palms overlooking the bay. Part of the boardwalk also takes you out over the water. As the bay is shallow and quite clear, you'll have no trouble spotting the bottom.

Swiftcurrent Lake, Glacier National Park: The first 0.6 miles of the trail at this Montana park heads through an evergreen forest with several short spur trails leading to beaches along Swiftcurrent Lake. Meltwater from Grinnell Glacier feeds the lake, making for an crystal clear albeit cold water.

Leigh Lake, Grand Teton National Park: Several alpine lakes perfect for a family outing sit at the Wyoming park's central String Lake Area. The 1.8-mile round trip trail heads around a shimmering blue lake through green pines with gray Mount Moran soaring in the background. During summer, enjoy a picnic on the beach and then a swim in the cool waters.

Ruby Beach Trail, Olympic National Park: The Washington park's Pacific Ocean shoreline features gushing sea stacks, piles of driftwood logs, and colorful, wave-polished stones. To enjoy all three, take the 1.4-mile Ruby Beach Trail. Some of the driftwood here has floated in from the distant Columbia River.

Coastal Trail, Redwood National Park: With more than 40 miles of pristine Pacific Ocean coastline, the northern California park is the perfect place to see tide pools and sea stacks. The latter are visible from many highway vistas but to get close up to a tide pool – a small body of saltwater that sustains many colorful sea creatures on the beach at low tide – explore the 1-mile segment (2-miles round trip) of the Coastal Trail at Enderts Beach south of Crescent City.

Fall colors

Ah, autumn – the world appears to have been repainted, as red, gold and sienna orange leaves contrast with the blue sky. For many travelers, fall is their favorite time to hit the road.

But there's more to see than the leaves. As they fall to the ground, the landscape opens up, allowing you to spot interesting geological features or terrain that summer's green foliage keeps hidden. More animal sightings also are possible as birds migrate while mammals gorge in preparation for winter's cold.

America's national parks offer a number of great places to experience autumn's beauty. And with summer vacation over, many of the parks will be less crowded.

Six national parks particularly deliver great autumn experiences for travelers.

Cuyahoga Falls National Park: Brandywine Falls ranks among the most popular of the Ohio park's several waterfalls. The area surrounding the falls is gorgeous in October beneath autumn leaves, and the Brandywine Gorge Trail to it is shaded

Cedar Creek and Abbey Island at Ruby Beach, Olympic National Park.

almost the entire way by red maples and eastern hemlocks. With a combination of segments from the Stanford Road Metro Parks Bike and Hike Trail, the gorge trail loops 1.5 miles to the falls then back to the trailhead with several crossings of Brandywine Creek.

Great Sand Dunes National Park: Most people visit this Colorado park for the sand dunes soaring 60-plus stories in the sky. There's more to the park than dunes, though. The Montville Trail provides an excellent sample of that as it heads into the surrounding mountains. The 0.5-mile loop partially runs alongside a creek, where the golden canopy of cottonwood and aspen trees sends you to an autumn wonderland.

Great Smoky Mountains National Park: The 1-mile round trip Clingmans Dome Trail heads to the highest spot in the national park and Tennessee. Autumn leaves on the road to Clingmans Dome usually change about mid-October, offering a spectacular red, orange and yellow display. At the dome's top, views of those swaths of harvest colors can stretch for up to a hundred miles in all directions.

Hot Springs National Park: Though hardly thought of as a backcountry wilderness experience, the Arkansas park does offer a number of forested trails to enjoy. The best in autumn is the Hot Springs Mountain Trail. Heading through a beautiful mixed hardwood and pine forest, the route offers a gorgeous fall leaf display – and cooler temperatures than during muggy summer.

Shenandoah National Park: Spectacular autumn views await day hikers on the Stony Man Trail, a segment of the Appalachian National Scenic Trail. At the trail's top, you'll be rewarded with an expansive view of the Shenandoah Valley and the Massanutten and Allegheny Mountains beyond, their trees alit in harvest colors, as you breathe in clean, crisp air.

Death Valley National Park – OK, there are no autumn leaves here at all – but September's cooler temperatures ensure you actually can step out of an air conditioned vehicle for much longer than a minute to experience the forbidding desert landscape. Among the best places in the California park to visit is the Golden Canyon Interpretive Trail, where you can learn to read rocks that tell the tale of how a lake once here vanished.

Romance

What are the most romantic places in the world? Paris? Hawaii? Italy?

Try a national park.

Though national parks often are thought of as places to get back to nature, they're also great spots to get a little closer to your sweetie. Among the romantic possibilities are moonbows, romantic vistas, desert oasis and incredible sunrises.

49 Palms Oasis, Joshua Tree National Park.

Moonbow over waterfalls: At night during a full moon, moonbows often can be seen over waterfalls as the silvery light from Earth's nearest heavenly body refracts off the mist. Plan a spring or early summer visit to Yosemite National Park when the moon is full. On a clear night, moonbows – the moon's light reflected off water droplets – can span 2425-foot high Yosemite Fall with a trail leading right to its base.

Desert oasis: What is more romantic than midnight at the oasis? Joshua Tree National Park has a few, with the 49 Palms Oasis among the easiest to reach. The 49 Palms Oasis Trail heads 1.5-miles to stands of fan palms and water pools. Bring a blanket to lay out on the sand and a picnic basket for an evening snack under the stars.

Breathtaking vistas: For many, vistas of the Blue Ridge Mountains rank among the nation's most beautiful natural

Sunrise at Pu'u'ula'ula Summit, Haleakalā National Park.

scenery. The 4-mile hike up to the summit of Old Rag Mountain via the Ridge Trail at Shenandoah National Park is challenging, but the 360 degree view from the top is unparalleled, as nearly 200,000 acres of wilderness stretch below you. Twirl your beloved around in a dance so that the entire scene spins before her eyes.

Stargazing: Boasting among the darkest skies in continental America, you can see up to 7,500 stars with the naked eye – nearly four times more than is typical in a rural area – at Bryce Canyon National Park. The Piracy Point Trail, a half-mile round trip from Far View Point, leads to a picnic area overlooking a cliff perfect for stargazing. Study up on the names of a few stars in the night sky and point them out to your sweetheart.

Fruitpicking: The Park Service at Capitol Reef National Park maintains more than 3,100 trees – including cherry, apricot, peach, pear and apple – in orchards planted decades ago by Mormon pioneers. For a small fee, park visitors can pick the fruit when in season. While there's no designated trail, the Historic Fruita Orchards Walk takes you through the fruit trees near Utah Hwy. 24. Share with your beloved what you've picked at your next rest stop.

Sunrise to propose by: At 10,023 feet, Pu'u'ula'ula Summit at Haleakalā National Park offers what many consider the world's most romantic sunrise. As the sun ascends over a blanket of clouds below the summit, it colors the crater from the inside out in an incredible light show. Bring a breakfast picnic and as the new day begins, propose marriage, for the sunrise symbolizes the dawning of your life together. Since you can drive to the summit, after she says "Yes," together hike one of the trails into the crater (either the Keonehe'ehe'e Trail or the Halemau'u Trail).

Sunrises and sunsets

Nothing quite so effectively displays Mother Nature's beauty than a sunrise or sunset, those few moments each day when the world shines golden and with incredible serenity.

Some of America's best sunrises and sunsets can be seen in her national parks. They range from the where the morning light first touches America each day to romantic sunsets over tropical waters, from the subtle signal for a million bats to begin their day to incredible sunrises over the continent's deepest chasm.

Here are seven must-see sunrises and sunsets at our national parks.

First sunrise at Acadia National Park: Day hikers can walk to one of the first spots where the sun touches America each morning via the South Ridge Trail in Maine's Acadia National

Park. The trail is a 7.2-miles round trip to the top of Cadillac Mountain, which is the highest summit on the Eastern seaboard. Though the hike would be done in the dark, with moonglow and flashlights, the trail is traversable. Acadia's ancient granite peaks are among the first places in the United States where the sunrise can be seen. Be sure to bring a blanket to lay out on the cold rock and take a seat looking southeast.

Gold-lined paths at Bryce Canyon: Fairyland really does exist – it's smack dab in southcentral in Utah, where a maze of totem pole-like rock formations called hoodoos grace Bryce Canyon National Park. Hoodoos are unusual landforms in which a hard caprock slows the erosion of the softer mineral beneath it. The result is a variety of fantastical shapes. Take the Queens Garden Trail, which descends into the fantasyland of hoodoos. When hiking during the early morning, sunrise's orange glow magically lights the trail's contours.

Rock monoliths aglow at Zion: A fantastic view of Zion National Park's famous Beehives, East Temple, the Streaked Wall, and the Towers of the Virgin, await on the Canyon Overlook Trail. Sunrise is a particularly good time to make the hike as the trail heads west with the sun behind you casting the rock formations in an orange glow that steadily brightens with each passing moment. The Altar of Sacrifice, Sundial and West Temple – collectively known as the Towers of the Virgin – are particularly impressive. They sit directly west of the short trail's vista.

Breathtaking light show at Grand Canyon: Among the Grand Canyon National Park's most spectacular sights – sunrise and sunset – can be seen within walking distance of Grand Canyon Village in Arizona. While the South Rim Trail extends several miles along the canyon edge, you only have to walk to Mather Point, where views of the canyon shift like pictures in a

Hoodoo rock formations at Bryce Canyon ampitheater.

marquee at both sunrise and sunset. Another great spot that's a little less crowded is Ooh Ahh Point on the South Kaibab Trail, which is east of the village and south of Yaki Point. The aptly named Ooh Ahh Point is less than 200 feet below the rim.

100-mile views at Great Smoky Mountains: You can enjoy views of sunrises and sunsets with rays covering up to a hundred miles on the Clingmans Dome Trail in Great Smoky Mountains National Park. How incredible are the sunsets? They can be crowded, as those hoping to photograph the stunning scenery line up 45 minutes before the sun descends.

Romantic sunsets at Biscayne National Park: A full 95 percent of Florida's Biscayne National Park sits underwater, a turquoise blue paradise laced with vividly colored coral reefs – and nothing quite says romance like a sunset over this tropical ocean. Adams Key offers a quarter-mile trail from the dock through the hardwood hammock on the island's west side; most of the route skirts the beach, where the sunset can be enjoyed.

Needles aglow at Canyonlands National Park: Clambering over boulders and ambling across strangely angled slickrock – and watching needles aglow at sunset – await on Canyonlands National Park's Slickrock Trail in southeastern Utah. The 2.9-mile loop trail generally follows a mesa rim. Plan to walk the trail about an hour or so before sunset; on the final mile, tall thin rock formations called needles fill the horizon, glowing crimson as the sun sets.

Vistas

Certainly the best memories of any trip are the great vistas enjoyed along the way. For some, the beauty of the natural scene before them ranks far above any man-made art. For others, the diminutiveness experienced upon seeing an incredible panorama is a spiritual moment.

America's national parks fortunately preserve the most impressive of these vistas. Some offer dramatic desert scenes of changing rock colors while others deliver awe-inspiring autumn rainbows of leaves. One even lets you gaze into an otherwordly basin of hot springs.

Great Smoky Mountains National Park, Clingmans Dome: You can enjoy views of up to a hundred miles atop one of the highest points east of the Mississippi River. The 1-mile round trip Clingmans Dome Trail heads to the highest spot in Great Smoky Mountains National Park and Tennessee and the third tallest east of the Mississippi. The top rewards with an incredible 360 degree panorama. A verdant spruce-fir forest sits at the ridge tops while in autumn the leaves of hardwoods below adds swaths of harvest colors. On clear days, 100-mile views are possible.

Grand Canyon National Park, South Rim: Perhaps the

South Rim, Grand Canyon National Park.

most fantastic vista in all of North America is the Grand Canyon's South Rim. Indeed, the Grand Canyon rightly defies description. Most who see it for the first time say it reminds them of a majestic painting, appropriately suggesting it's a place that only can be visualized by actually gazing at it. While the South Rim Trail extends several miles along the canyon edge, a short section east of the El Tovar Hotel offers the best views. You'll be able to see the Colorado River a mile below and an array of incredible buttes, towers and ridges and that stretch up to 10 miles away to the canyon's other side.

Yosemite National Park, Yosemite Valley: Two sweeping views of Yosemite Valley await on the Sentinel Dome and Taft Point Loop. Located south of the valley along Glacier Point Road, the trail runs 4.9-miles. Taft Point allows you to get right up to the edge of the valley rim, offering magnificent views of

Yosemite Valley below and Yosemite Fall (the tallest in North America) and El Capitan across the way. The 360 degree views from the top of Sentinel Dome – which peaks at 8127 feet – are the hike's highlight. Among the visible sights are Yosemite Valley, Half Dome, El Capitan, Yosemite Falls, North Dome, and Basket Dome.

Yellowstone National Park, Fairy Falls Trail: The multicolored Grand Prismatic Spring and an array of geysers can be seen on the first 0.6 miles of Yellowstone's Fairy Falls Trail. A 400-foot stretch of the trail appropriately known as Picture Hill provides a grand vista of the spring. About 370 feet in diameter, Grand Prismatic is the largest hot spring in the United States and the third largest in the world. It reaches a depth of 121 feet. Be sure to bring polarized sunglasses. By wearing them, you can see the spring's rainbow colors reflected in the steam rising off the water. The smaller Excelsior Geyser Crater sits beyond the geological wonder.

Zion National Park, Canyon Overlook Trail: You can hike past hoodoos to a vista that affords a fantastic view of Zion National Park's famous Beehives, East Temple, the Streaked Wall, and the Towers of the Virgin, on the Canyon Overlook Trail. The 1-mile round trip of pinnacles, arches and domes feels like a walk on an alien world straight out of a science fiction film. Summer temps are cooler in the morning and late evening.

Mesa Verde National Park, Park Point: Park Point, Mesa Verde's highest spot at 8572 feet above sea level with 360 degree views, is often touted as the most impressive vista in the United States. The 0.5-mile round trip Park Point Overlook Trail takes you to the view of Montezuma and Mancos valleys, and on a clear day, you can see four states – Colorado, Utah, Arizona and New Mexico. Add 0.5-miles round trip to the fire lookout tower for additional great views.

Yosemite Falls, Yosemite National Park.

Waterfalls

Nothing quite demonstrates the awesome power and beauty of Mother Nature like a waterfall – hundreds of gallons of water rushing several stories over a cliffside, the vertical stream nestled in lush greenery, the mist and droplets that splash on you at the fall's base.

Fortunately, several of our national parks preserve many of the country's most fantastic falls. Most of them are quite easy to reach via short hikes.

Yosemite Falls: If there is one waterfall that everyone absolutely must see, it's this one in California's Yosemite National Park. Actually consisting of seven waterfalls, Yosemite Falls sends water rushing 2,425 feet downward into the valley. Depending on snow melt, the falls' peak flow typically occurs in May when up to 2,400 gallons of water flow down Yosemite Falls every second.

You can hike 1.2-miles round trip to the base of North America's tallest waterfall. During spring, you may want to take the trail on a clear night when the moon is full, especially if on a romantic trip. Moonlit rainbows – called moonbows – span the waterfalls.

Queenie and Fido also can enjoy the waterfalls, as leashed dogs are allowed on the trail. Be sure that your dog is comfortable with crowds and other people, however.

Tokopah Falls: Not many travelers have heard of Tokopah Falls, but it's an incredible sight. A series of cascades, it drops 1200 feet – almost the height of the Empire State Building – at California's Sequoia National Park. It's a park of tall trees and tall waterfalls. A glacier carved Tokopah Valley, leaving high gray cliff walls that cradle a meadow, creeks, and a pine and fir forest. The 3.8-mile (600 foot elevation gain) Tokopah Falls Trail leads to its namesake, which is the park's highest waterfall.

Avalanche Lake waterfalls: With melting glaciers and high mountains, waterfalls can be found aplenty in Montana's Glacier National Park. Melting glaciers feed several lakes across the park, including Avalanche Lake. Start on the Trail of the Cedars then turn off onto the Avalanche Lake Trail. The 4.7-miles round trip (505-foot gain) trail heads to Avalanche Lake, where several waterfalls from Sperry Glacier drop several hundred feet to fill the valley with its turquoise waters.

Hidden Falls: You can enjoy this waterfall and then a vista at 7200 feet elevation on Grand Teton National Parks' Hidden Falls-Inspiration Point Trail. The trail runs 3.8-miles round trip into Cascade Canyon. Though technically not a waterfall but a series of cascades running 200 feet over several multiple steps, Wyoming's Hidden Falls still impresses. Because only part of the cascades are steep, there's a lot of confusion among various sources about exactly how high the drop that looks most like

Hidden Falls, Grand Teton National Park.

a waterfall actually is – some say 80 feet and others say 100. Afterward, visit Inspiration Point, a short walk from the falls.

Fairy Falls: The trail to Fairy Falls at Yellowstone National Park offers a three-for-one deal: the multi-colored Grand Prismatic Spring, an array of geysers, and a 197-foot waterfall. If going to see Old Faithful, this is a perfect nearby trail to hike the same day. The 5.6-mile hike begins with geysers then arrives Grand Prismatic Spring, a wonder that boasts multicolored rings of algae. Fairy Falls comes next. The waterfalls' base supports a variety of vegetation. If looking for a place to picnic, the rocks downstream from the falls where raspberry bushes grow makes a perfect spot.

Marymere Falls: A trail through a lush, old growth forest that ends at this waterfall will delight anyone hiking the Marymere Falls Trail at Olympic National Park in Washington. The 1.6-mile round trip trail really is like taking two entirely different hikes in one. Most of the trail heads through an intensely green Pacific Northwest rain forest while the last portion at the destination is purely about the waterfalls. Marymere Falls is about 90 feet high, and you'll get really close to it as the trail passes the small plunge pool. Hikers also can take a stairs to see the falls' upper segment. A few landings on the stairs offers fantastic views of the falls from different angles.

Laurel Falls: Though Rainbow Falls is the tallest at Great Smoky Mountains National Park, many visitors pass it up because of the strenuous hike. One that's much easier to reach and still spectacular in its own right is 80-foot Laurel Falls. The Laurel Falls Trail runs 2.6-miles round trip through a pine-oak woods with hemlock and beech along the stream, making for a colorful walk in autumn. May also is impressive, as mountain laurel blooms along the trail and near the falls, which runs its highest that month. Deer, often with fawns, wood squirrels, and songbirds are common on the trail. The waterfall on Laurel Branch consists of an upper and a lower section. A wide walkway crosses the stream where the mist from the falls roils overhead.

Brandywine Falls: This 65-foot waterfalls awaits visitors on the Brandywine Gorge Trail at Ohio's Cuyahoga Valley National Park. The Brandywine Gorge Trail loops 1.5 miles to the falls then back to the trailhead with several crossings of Brandywine Creek. The area surrounding the falls is gorgeous in October beneath autumn leaves, but the trail can be hiked any season. It's shaded almost the entire way by red maples with eastern hemlocks and green moss upon the ground once closer to the falls.

Wildflowers
From rare California poppies to sweet-scented phlox, wild-

Catawba rhododendron blooms, Great Smoky Mountains National Park.

flowers begin to bloom each spring across much of the country. Filling green meadows, desert basins, and forest floors, wildflowers bring a special beauty that usually can only be seen for a few weeks.

Our national parks rank among the best places to enjoy wildflowers. As those parks cover wide swaths of protected land, they offer ample area for massive blooms, enhancing the already beautiful scenery.

Here are six not-to-miss spots at our national parks for spotting wildflowers from March through summer.

Pinnacles National Park: Each spring, brilliant orange California poppies, lavender-colored bush lupine, and white mariposa lilies blossom across the nation's newest national park. To see a variety of them at different elevations and from a number of vistas, take the High Peaks and Bear Gulch trails.

Great Smoky Mountains National Park: About the same time on the other side of the continent, the forest floor on the Mingus Creek Trail turns fragrant with the pleasant sent of blue phlox. Several other shade-loving flowers also can be found along the creek, including violets, Virginia bluebells and white trillium. During late April, expect to see flame azalea in bloom on the Deep Creek/Indian Falls trails. In May, look for mountain laurel, and in June for rhododendron.

Glacier National Park: From late June through early August, summer wildflower blooms are at their peak. Check out the Swiftcurrent Lake Loop Trail for meadows strewn with purple asters, white torch-shaped clusters of beargrass, and sun yellow glacier lilies, all with majestic mountains as a backdrop.

Sequoia National Park: Next to the world's largest trees are blossoms that somehow manage to stand out despite their comparative size. On the Crescent Meadow Trail in early July, lavender Mustang clover with yellow centers look like little pins of brilliant light against the immense pine cones that have fallen into the grass.

Crater Lake National Park: Wildflowers usually bloom along the stream next to the Annie Creek Trail and across the meadows from mid-July through August. Among those that might be spotted are Macloskey's violet, big huckleberry, sulphur flower, Crater Lake currant, western mountain ash, and wax currant.

Great Basin National Park: Amid the high desert is an oasis of summer wildflowers on the Alpine Lakes Trail. Spring-fed Lehman Creek flows into a lake and supports Parry's primrose, penstemon, and phlox, all set against vibrant green grass. Butterflies are abundant here as well.

Wildlife
America's national parks are known for their great vistas and fantastic rock formations, but they also preserve another treasure: wildlife.

Bison at Lamar Valley, Yellowstone National Park.

In fact, national parks rank among the best places to see interesting and rare wildlife. Late summer marks a particularly good time for wildlife viewing at many parks as most mothers bring out their young that time of the year.

Given the breadth of national park locations, there's also the opportunity to see almost every kind of North American wildlife, from those that live on mountains, in marine environments, and in the tropics to those that make their homes on prairies, deserts and in temperate forests.

Mountains: Travelers can explore the "Serengeti of North America" on the Lamar Valley Trail at Wyoming's Yellowstone National Park. Like the mountain-ringed African plain, Lamar Valley serves as home to the classic megafauna that define North America. Bison, elk, grizzlies, black bears, wolves, coyotes, eagles, osprey and more all can be found at this high elevation. Coyotes also can be seen wandering about, looking for a meal while bald eagles and osprey grace the skies. Grizzlies reside in the hilly woods, but they and the area's other big two predators – black bears and wolf packs – prefer to remain under cover than be seen.

Marine: You can encounter an array of marine wildlife on the Beach Trail at Alaska's Glacier Bay National Park. Low tide also provides an opportunity to see intertidal life. As the waters retreat into the ocean – and water levels here can fall 25 vertical feet, among the greatest extremes in the world – a number of animals and plants are exposed. Don't be surprised to spot starfish and snails on the sands and grasses. On shore, a variety of sea birds gather and fly over, often nabbing exposed intertidal creatures for a meal. During those first moments of sunlight, watch for humpback whales, harbor porpoise, puffins, sea otters, and Steller sea lions, frolicking and feeding in the mouth of the bay. Bring binoculars. If lucky, you'll also hear the blow of humpback whales.

Tropics: Tropical wildlife can be safely seen from the Anhinga Trail at Florida's Everglades National Park. The trail's boardwalk takes you over open water where you can watch for alligators peeking out of a river, as well as turtles, herons and egrets. Winter marks the best season to see the most wildlife. A number of birds spend their time in the Everglades after migrating from a northern clime. Among those you can spot are the double breasted cormorant, great egret, great blue heron, snowy egret, tricolored heron, white ibis and woodstork. Turkey vultures congregate in the marsh during the early morning hours.

Prairies: North America's largest mammal – the bison – freely roams North Dakota's Theodore Roosevelt National Park, and the Buckhorn Trail is an excellent place to spot them and other Great Plains wildlife. The trail includes a prairie dog

The majestic anhinga inhabits Everglades National Park.

town that stretches for about a mile. You'll be able to spot them barking from their burrow entrances as they keep an eye out for predators. Hawks, coyotes and rattlesnakes are among the creatures hoping to make an unsuspecting prairie dog its dinner.

Deserts: Among the best spots to see desert wildlife is the beautiful Painted Desert Trail at Petrified National Forest. At dawn and dusk, pronghorn and mule deer graze while coyotes, kit foxes and bobcats stalk prey such as black-tailed jackrabbit, desert cottontail, various squirrels, and pocket gophers. Overhead, watch for red-tailed hawks and kestrels circling in search of a meal. Burrowing owls, roadrunners, and quail stick to the ground. Of course, there are small, harmless lizards darting about the rocks. Among them is are the colorful collared lizard with its bright green body and yellow feet.

Temperate forests: Great Smoky Mountains National Park, though stretching across the Appalachian Mountains, offers the opportunity to see many of the animals that reside in temperate forests covering much of the continent east of the Mississippi River. The Deep Creek/Indian Falls trails in the park's North Carolina section sports Eastern cottontail rabbit, groundhogs, river otter, and white-tailed deer. Also present but much more elusive, as they keep to themselves, are black bear, bobcat, coyote, red fox, red wolf, and wild boar.

Winter

Most travelers think of summer as the best time to hit national parks – but winter also offers several spectacular sights that make for memorable visits.

So when the snow starts falling, consider a road trip to one of the following parks.

Birders paradise: Winter marks the best time to hike Florida's Everglades National Park, as the subtropical climate means unbearably hot and buggy summers. Indeed, a number of birds already know this and spend their time in the Everglades after migrating from a northern clime. Among those you can spot on the Anhinga Trail are the double breasted cor-

Golden Canyon, Death Valley National Park.

morant, great egret, great blue heron, snowy egret, tricolored heron, white ibis and woodstork; turkey vultures congregate during the early morning hours.

Wildlife sightings: Leafless trees and snow's white backdrop makes sighting large wildlife a lot easier in winter than summer. The Warner Point Nature Trail on the south rim of Colorado's Black Canyon of the Gunnison National Park offers the chance to spot elk and Rocky Mountain bighorn sheep. Look for the elk in clearings and the bighorn sheep on the rocky cliff sides.

Heavy waterfalls: At most parks, waterfalls are most active in spring and early summer, thanks to snow melt. Not so at Washington state's Olympic National Park. Rain is more likely there during winter, meaning the water flow is higher, making for a more spectacular creeks and falls. One good trail through the park's lush, old growth forest that ends at a waterfall is the Marymere Falls Trail.

Bearable heat: During summer, oppressive heat makes California's Death Valley National Park at best a pass through seen from a motor vehicle. The park's average high in January is a pleasant 67 degrees, though, making winter the perfect time to walk the foreboding desert landscape. Among those sights is the lowest point in North America. Badwater Basin sits 282 feet below sea level and can be accessed in a mile-long round trip hike.

Avoid the crowds: Visitation drops during winter at most parks, so the trade-off for bundling up in coat, cap and gloves is seeing the great scenery without all of the crowds. A good bet is Yosemite National Park's spectacular Yosemite Valley in California. The Lower Yosemite Fall Trail offers a number of fantastic views of Yosemite Falls in a 1.2-mile loop with the added coolness of falling water frozen in mid-flight on the granite rocks.

Christmas

A little secret: Among the best ways to escape holiday stress is a national park trip. Though often thought of as a summer destination, only a couple of the parks close in winter, and almost all offer warm, cozy and peaceful holiday experiences. A bonus is that almost all parks are less crowded during winter.

Here are five great holiday-themed must-do's at our national parks.

Winter wonderland, Yellowstone National Park: Book a getaway at the Old Faithful Snow Lodge, which can only be reached this time of year by snow coach or snowmobile. The Christmas-decorated lodge keeps its fireplace burning with plenty of hot cocoa for visitors. During the day, hike past "ghost

Christmas caroling in the cavern, Mammoth Cave National Park.

trees," formed when the steam from the Old Faithful geyser freezes on pine tree needles. Bison with snow-covered manes often feed across the geyser valley.

Polar Express train ride, Cuyahoga Valley National Park: Each December prior to Christmas, the Cuyahoga Valley Scenic Railroad's Polar Express chugs through the scenic Ohio park. Among the highlights on the refurbished passenger train is a reading of the children's book "Polar Express," which inspired a movie and this trip. Many passengers ride the train in their pajamas! If in the Southwest, a private company also runs a Polar Express to Grand Canyon National Park.

Luminaria-lit skiing: Denali National Park: Every December, rangers light the small paper lanterns that line ski trails at the Alaska park. Visitors also can snowshoe or stroll the route, which leaves from the Murie Science and Learning

Center, Denali's Winter Visitor Center. Several other National Park Service sites offering luminaria displays and hikes including Florida's De Soto National Memorial and Arizona's Tonto National Monument.

Snowshoe wildlife hike, Rocky Mountain National Park: Ranger-led snowshoe tours take visitors of this Colorado park to a variety of wildlife, including elk, coyotes, deer and snowshoe hares. The trail is utterly quiet as snow-capped mountains and evergreens rise around you on all sides.

Caroling in a cave, Mammoth Cave National Park: In early December, the Kentucky park holds Christmas carol sing-ing in the world's longest cave system. It's a tradition that goes back to 1883 when local residents held the first Christmas celebration in the cave's passageways.

Historical sites

While the National Park Service's 62 major parks largely focus on protecting natural wonders and wilderness, they also preserve several historical sites. Though many are merely ruins, others are in just as good of shape (if not better) than when they originally stood.

Historic Fort Jefferson: At Dry Tortugas National Park, you can visit a fort used during the Civil War. Built with more than 16 million bricks during the mid-1800s, Fort Jefferson is the Western Hemisphere's largest masonry structure. Six walls and towers with a moat make up the fort's outer area on Garden Key.

19th Century Mining Town: Crossing a thick rolling woodland, the Colorado River Trail at Rocky Mountain National Park offers nice views of Colorado River, arguably the Southwest's most important waterway. The trail to the ruins of an 19th century mining town, Lulu City, in a 6.2-miles round trip with 320-

John Oliver cabin in Cades Cove, Great Smoky Mountains National Park.

foot elevation gain.

Appalachian life: A number of great day hikes allow visitors to explore the Great Smoky Mountain National Park's rich history. Pioneer cabins, churches and mills await on sev-eral short day hikes, including those at Cades Code and Mingus Mill.

Ancient native ruins: Among the largest cliff dwellings ever constructed hundreds of years ago by the Ancient Puebloans, also known as the Anasazi, is Mesa Verde National Park's Cliff Palace. It contains 150 rooms and 23 kivas constructed of sandstone, mortar and wooden beams. The 0.25-mile round trip hike only can be done via a ranger-guided tour. Tickets typicaly must be purcahsed an hour ahead of the guided tour time.

Trees

Among the most fantastic sights at our national parks are

trees. Whether they be gigantic, fossilized, or older than the hills (figuratively speaking), they're certain to awe. Here are six great tree sites to visit.

Sequoias: Your family will feel like hobbits walking through scenes from "The Lord of the Rings" movies on the General Grant Tree Trail at Kings Canyon National Park. The 0.5-mile trail heads through the General Grant Grove of giant sequoias. More than 120 sequoias in the grove exceed 10 feet in diameter and most tower several stories over your head.

Redwoods: Hiking families can enjoy a trip into what feels like the forest primeval on a segment of the Damnation Creek Trail in Redwood National Park. For those with younger children, a 1.2-mile round trip through just the redwoods section of the trail makes for more than an incredible, inspiring walk.

Bristlecone pines: On several of Great Basin National Park's glacial moraines rise incredibly ancient bristlecone pines, many nearly 5,000 years old, meaning they began growing as the ancient Egyptians built the pyramids. The 2.8-mile round trip Bristlecone Pine Trail allows you to walk among a grove of the trees, which scientists say likely are the oldest living organisms on Earth.

Joshua trees: Day hikers can enjoy a walk through a large Joshua tree forest in the desert above the Palm Springs, Calif., area. A segment of the Boy Scout Trail at Joshua Tree National Park runs through a grove for a 2.4-mile round trip. Technically not a tree, the unusual Joshua tree is a member of the lily family.

Chestnut trees: Day hikers can head through what used to be a grove of majestic chestnut trees. The Cades Cove Nature Trail runs 1.4-miles round trip trail (from the parking lot) and sits in Cades Cove, an isolated mountain valley that is a popular destination thanks to many well-preserved structures from

Base of General Grant Tree, Kings Canyon National Park.

pioneer days. A few seedlings of the great chestnut remain.

Petrified forest: Families can hike the remains of a woodlands dating from the dinosaurs' earliest days on the Great Logs Trail in Petrified Forest National Park. The fairly easy walk consists of two loops that combine for a 0.6-mile round trip. Because of the hot Arizona weather, spring and autumn mark the best time to hike the trail.

Learn more about these and many other great national park trails in the author's "Best Sights to See at America's National Parks."

About the Author

Rob Bignell is a long-time hiker, editor, and author of the popular "Best Sights to See," "Hikes with Tykes," "Headin' to the Cabin," and "Hittin' the Trail" guidebooks and several other titles. He and his son Kieran have been hiking together for more than a decade. Rob has served as an infantryman in the Army National Guard and taught middle school students in New Mexico and Wisconsin. His newspaper work has won several national and state journalism awards, from editorial writing to sports reporting. In 2001, *The Prescott Journal*, which he served as managing editor of, was named Wisconsin's Weekly Newspaper of the Year. Rob and Kieran live in Wisconsin.

CHECK OUT ALL THESE GREAT HIKING BOOKS BY THE AUTHOR

"Best Sights to See" series:
- America's National Parks
- Great Smoky Mountain National Park
- Indiana Dunes National Park
- Joshua Tree National Park
- Rocky Mountain National Park
- Voyageurs National Park

"Hikes with Tykes" series:
- Hikes with Tykes: A Practical Guide to Day Hiking with Children
- Hikes with Tykes: Games and Activities

"Headin' to the Cabin" series:
- Day Hiking Trails of Northeast Minnesota
- Day Hiking Trails of Northwest Wisconsin

"Hittin' the Trail" series:
National parks
- Grand Canyon National Park (ebook only)
California
- Palm Springs and the Coachella Valley
Minnesota
- Gooseberry Falls State Park
- Split Rock Lighthouse State Park
Minnesota/Wisconsin
- Interstate State Park
- St. Croix National Scenic Riverway

Wisconsin
- Barron County
- Bayfield County
- Best Autumn Hikes
- Burnett County (ebook only)
- Chippewa Valley (Eau Claire, Chippewa, Dunn, Pepin counties)
- Crex Meadows Wildlife Area (ebook only)
- Douglas County
- Polk County
- St. Croix County
- Sawyer County
- Washburn County

GET CONNECTED!

Follow the author to learn about other great trails and for useful hiking tips:

- Blog: *hikeswithtykes.blogspot.com*
- Facebook: *dld.bz/fBq2C*
- Pinterest: *pinterest.com/rbignell41*
- Twitter: *twitter.com/dayhikingtrails*
- Website: *dayhikingtrails.wordpress.com*

If you enjoyed this book,
please take a few moments to write a review of it.
https://tinyurl.com/y6yzpn4r
Thank you!

www.ingramcontent.com/pod-product-compliance
Lightning Source LLC
Chambersburg PA
CBHW060936040426
42445CB00011B/885